Maggie Beer is one of Australia's best-known cooks. In addition to co-hosting *The Cook and The Chef* and making regular appearances on *MasterChef Australia*, Maggie devotes her time to the Farmshop in the Barossa Valley, where it all began, and to her Export Kitchen, which produces her famous range of pates, fruit pastes, jams, sauces and verjuice, and develops her range of super-indulgent ice creams.

Maggie is the author of nine successful cookbooks, *Maggie's Christmas*, *Maggie Beer (Lantern Cookery Classics)*, *Maggie's Verjuice Cookbook*, *Maggie's Kitchen*, *Maggie's Harvest*, *Maggie's Table*, *Cooking with Verjuice*, *Maggie's Orchard* and *Maggie's Farm*, and co-author of the bestselling *Stephanie Alexander & Maggie Beer's Tuscan Cookbook*.

Her website is maggiebeer.com.au
Visit the Maggie Beer Farm Shop on Instagram

Maggie's Kitchen

Maggie Beer

photography by Simon Griffiths

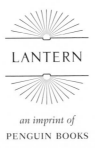

LANTERN

an imprint of
PENGUIN BOOKS

To the very special women of my family: my strong,
bossy, clever and chaotic daughters, Saskia and Elli.
And to my beloved granddaughters, Zoë, Lilly and Rory,
whom I suspect will become like their mothers in time.

Contents

Maggie's Kitchen Basics 1

Beginning 33

Middle 89

End 183

Index 239

Maggie's
Kitchen Basics

This book is all about sharing the things I believe you need to know to enjoy a good food life, from having the right equipment and choosing the finest ingredients to the cooking tips that are indispensable to achieving the best results.

I hope my ideas and recipes will expand your horizons and show how easy it is to enjoy simple food that is full of flavour every day of your life. I also hope that you will gain the confidence to deviate from my written words. To me, a recipe is like a road map – a starting point from which to work, a document that can accommodate your own likes and dislikes.

When it comes to deciding what to cook, rather than choosing a recipe and then heading off to shop for the listed ingredients, approach it the other way around. Go shopping and let yourself be seduced by whatever is in season, and then find a way to cook the produce that stands out most to you.

During the week, when time is tight, I generally grill or pan-fry a piece of meat, poultry or fish for dinner, with accompanying seasonal vegetables or salad alongside; the Crisp-skin Salmon on page 116 makes a regular appearance on my dinner table during such times. When things are less busy I like to make the most of longer cooking methods when, depending on the season, I might cook Pork Belly in Shiraz (see recipe page 128) or Pot-roasted Lamb Shoulder with Green Olives, Almonds and Apricots (see recipe page 164).

Equipment
I most use

Oven

I generally use a fan-forced oven. I guess I've used these since they became widely available in the early 80s as it made sense to me that they would circulate heat more evenly. Unless I've specified otherwise, all my oven temperatures are for using a fan-forced oven. If using a conventional (that is, non fan-forced) oven you may need to increase the temperature by 10 or 20°C (50 or 68°F). Get to know your oven, then decide whether whatever you are cooking needs to be rotated to compensate for any hot or cold spots in the specific oven used. I am lucky enough to also have a conventional non-fan-forced oven, which I use for cooking delicate things like meringues and custards or pâtés in a water bath. Fan-assisted ovens differ from fan-forced ovens in that use of the fan is optional, making them more flexible. Otherwise, you may want to look at European brands of multifunction ovens, which include conventional, fan-assisted and fan-forced settings in the same oven.

Refrigerator

In the main a household refrigerator runs at about 8–10°C (46–50°F), but even that is hard to say for certain. Look for a fridge with a thermometer fitted so you can gauge the temperature, which should be at 4°C (39°F) for highly perishable pâtés, seafood and poultry. Ideally, a fridge should also have warmer spots to keep cheeses and butter in peak condition and cooler spots for herbs and salad greens – a crisper with a thermometer attached would be perfect for these.

Whilst leftovers are somewhat inevitable, refrigeration dulls the flavour of most cooked food. Try to plan ahead so that – except in high summer or if you happen to live in the tropics – leftover chook from a lunchtime family roast can be used to make wonderful sandwiches for supper that night without having to be refrigerated in between, for example. Unless you have a glut on your hands, keep straw-berries and tomatoes out of the fridge, and even avocado too.

Baking equipment

- pastry brush
- rolling pin
- 24 cm tart tin with removable base
- round cake tins in a few sizes (I find that 22 cm and 24 cm are the ones I use most)
- 2 flat baking trays (scone trays are ideal)
- 2 medium-sized shallow baking dishes
- large rectangular baking dish (Pyrex or similar)
- large shallow baking dish (try to find the biggest one that wil fit into your oven – perfect for making a generous macaroni cheese or lasagne and roasting bones and vegetables for stock)
- 2 large bread tins
- wire racks for cooling cakes and tarts
- a large loaf tin

Knives and Slicers:

- good-quality forged-steel cook's knife (not too large)
- East/West knife (I use mine all the time. If you can only justify having one great cook's knife, then I recommend getting an East/West knife that feels right in your hand)
- vegetable paring knife
- selection of cheap serrated small knives (I find these very handy for tasks such as slicing tomatoes, cutting eggplant, segmenting citrus fruit, and picking vegetables from my garden)
- serrated bread knife
- good-quality knife sharpener that is easy to use
- flexible boning knife for filleting fish and removing sinew from meat
- oyster knife (if you are an oyster-lover)
- Stanley knife (optional), for scoring pork skin
- Japanese vegetable slicer or mandoline

Small utensils:

- digital meat thermometer
- a few kitchen timers (especially if you are as easily distracted as I)
- digital scales
- potato peeler (mine is by OXO Good Grips – it peels quinces beautifully too)
- top-quality pepper grinder that allows you to adjust the coarseness of the grind
- citrus zester with sharp 'claws' (I've even been known to take a lemon to the kitchenware shop to check before buying as there are so many blunt ones on the market)
- citrus juicer
- Microplane grater (see page 16)
- stainless steel box grater
- nutmeg grater
- mouli-legumes (also called a food mill) or potato ricer
- 2–3 pairs of easy-to-open tongs (including long tongs for the barbecue)
- 2–3 wooden spoons of different shapes and sizes
- 2 large solid stainless steel spoons
- 2 slotted stainless steel spoons
- soup ladle
- kitchen shears
- heat-resistant spatulas or pastry scrapers in a selection of sizes
- plastic pastry cutters for making pasta and gnocchi as well as pastries
- sieve that can double as a sifter
- set of stainless steel Australian standard metric measuring cups
- 2 sets of stainless steel Australian standard metric measuring spoons (mine are joined together); make sure that the tablespoon measure is for 20 ml and not the US 15 ml
- Australian standard metric measuring jug
- medium-sized whisk

Boards, trays and bowls

- 1 large bread board, plus a selection of wooden chopping boards
- 2–3 large plastic trays (especially useful when preparing and organising ingredients for entertaining)
- lots of glass or stainless steel mixing bowls – small, medium and large – that stack inside each other

Electrical equipment

- Magimix or other good-quality food processor
- electric mixer or hand-held electric beaters
- blender
- digital scales

Pots and pans:

- small saucepan with lid
- 2–3 medium-sized saucepans with lids
- large saucepan with lid
- stainless steel stockpot
- wide heavy-based saucepan for making risotto
- 3 non-stick frying pans – small, medium and large
- large, heavy-based, deep frying pan with a lid (preferably glass)
- omelette pan (or you can use the medium non-stick frying pan)
- char-grill pan (if you don't have a barbecue with a grill-plate)
- heavy-based cast-iron casserole (Le Creuset or similar)
- several roasting pans, both light and heavy-gauge

Choosing Pans

Choose an appropriately sized pan for the task at hand. When immersing ingredients in liquids, choose a pan in which the ingredients fit snugly so less liquid is required to cover them. Conversely, when pan-frying or deep-frying, it is best not to crowd the pan so that the food fries in the oil rather than poaches (which happens when the pan is overcrowded and the oil temperature consequently drops).

For pan-frying or poaching, I use a good-quality heavy-based non-stick frying pan. For roasting, I have both light- and heavy-gauge roasting pans with shallow sides that allow for good heat circulation (this factor being more important than the weight). For slow-cooking methods such as braising or stewing I use a heavy-based cast-iron casserole (mine is Le Creuset), since the meat can be first browned in this, then the weight of the pan and tight-fitting lid help to retain all of the natural juices, meaning that less liquid needs to be added.

Miscellaneous

- mortar and pestle
- salad spinner (invaluable for drying salad leaves and herbs)
- pasta machine (mine is made by Imperia and my grandchildren love using it too)
- plenty of Chux or other perforated dish cloths – I use these for many tasks other than just wiping benches, such as draining cheese and rubbing the skins off par-cooked baby carrots

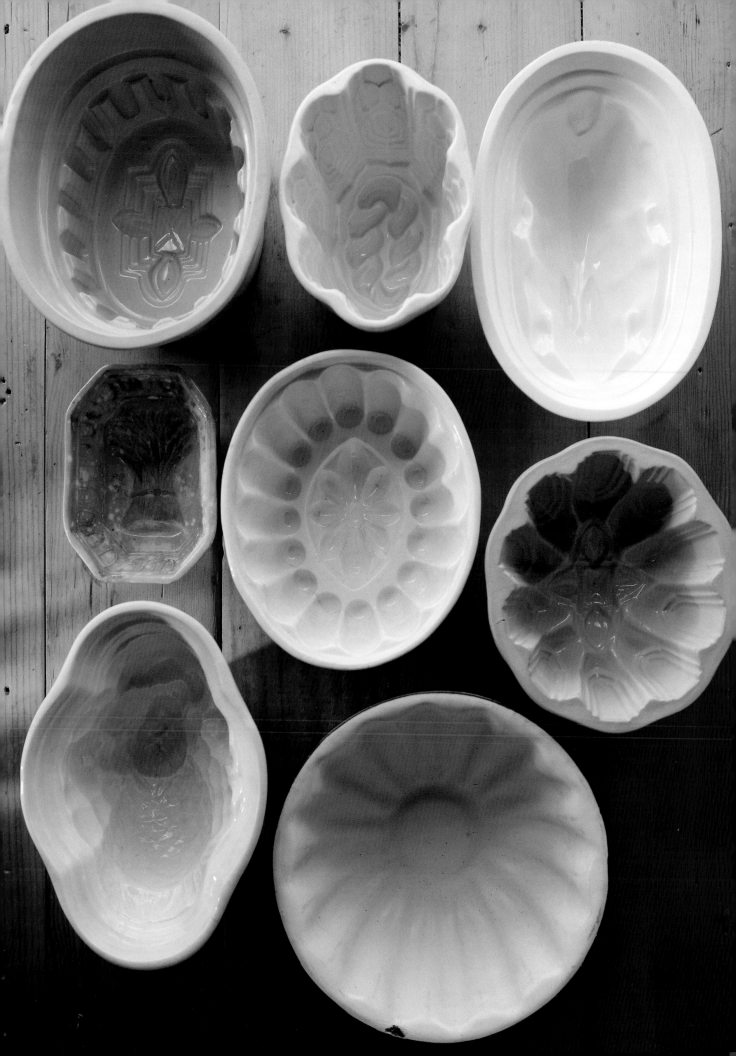

How I'd love a few modern things in my kitchen, like compartmentalised deep drawers to use as my larder, but I'm so emotionally attached to my old Barossa cupboards that I doubt I'll ever replace them. However, having a dark cupboard or pantry is good for storing extra virgin olive oils, chutneys, jams and most other pantry items, and clear air-tight containers are invaluable for storing grains, pulses or dried fruit.

The larder is such an important kitchen resource that I find it is the one cupboard in my house that is truly organised. This is especially vital for me, living in the country, as I don't have ready access to many of the store-cupboard ingredients I am so fussy about. For instance, when I buy artisan-made spelt pasta from Italy, I buy it by the carton. As a result I've needed to mouse-proof the store-cupboard I've started in my garden shed. I try so hard to keep this cupboard tidy (keeping baskets of similar ingredients grouped together such as the risotto rices with the polenta, spelt and freekeh), but it is rummaged through so frequently that I am forever having to give it a spring clean.

Dry goods larder

- extra virgin olive oil
- good sea salt flakes (I choose Murray River Salt Flakes as I like to support my local products; it is saltier than Maldon Sea Salt, still a benchmark of quality)
- verjuice (from the juice of unripe grapes)
- vino cotto (not only because I make this product which comes from the must of grapes, but also because I tend to use it instead of balsamic unless I've splurged on the finest – and oldest – aged balsamic I can afford at the time)
- authentic aged balsamic vinegar (labelled *Aceto Balsamico Tradizionale di Modena*)
- aged red-wine vinegar
- tomato sugo or passata
- tomato paste (try ones from Turkish or Persian supermarkets – they offer superb quality and are so inexpensive)
- tins of Italian peeled roma tomatoes (both whole and chopped)
- dried artisan-made pasta in a variety of shapes (made from both durum wheat and spelt)
- plain and self-raising flour
- polenta
- semolina
- burghul
- couscous

- freekeh
- risotto rice (I use Ferron-brand carnaroli)
- 45 g tins anchovies
- salted capers (I love using local ones produced by the Australian Caper Company in Mannum)
- dried currants
- raisins
- pitted prunes
- dried small Persian white figs
- dried apricots
- candied citrus peel
- sultanas

Spice larder

- cinnamon sticks
- dried Greek oregano (rigani)
- fresh Australian peppercorns (from the Australian pepper company, L and L Campagnolo Silkwood Pepper Farm in Queensland or a quality supplier such as Herbie's (herbies.com.au)
- juniper berries
- whole nutmeg
- saffron threads
- plump vanilla beans

In the freezer

- gel packs for transporting highly perishable food such as meat, poultry, seafood and pâté
- nuts (almonds, hazelnuts, pine nuts, walnuts), to prevent them from becoming rancid
- peas
- purchased puff pastry sheets (I use Carême Butter Puff Pastry)
- salmon fillets, with skin-on
- squid (whole)
- unsalted butter
- good-quality vanilla bean ice cream, made using real vanilla beans

Shopping and eating in tune with the seasons

At times it can be difficult to know which fruit and vegetables are in season because so many of them are available in stores year-round. Even onions have a natural season (which is from autumn to winter in the Barossa) and there are months when the current year's crop of dried onions will store no longer, so I have to wait for the new-season crop from Queensland, which I find are a totally different product.

If oranges, garlic or asparagus have been flown in from the USA, China or Chile it is because supermarkets think we want these products year-round. However, the more we ask supermarkets and greengrocers whether the produce on their shelves is Australian, how far it has travelled and when its natural season is, the more they will respond to this demand and provide information so we consumers can make informed decisions.

Produce in its natural season from our Australian farmers is what I want to buy (see the seasonal shopping lists on pages 12–13).

Choosing Fruit

Most fruit tastes best when eaten straight after being picked ripe from the tree. With a few exceptions, such as pears, which need to ripen off the tree, fruit doesn't ripen further after picking. Logistically this makes delivering fruit in its prime a hard task for the industry, given the distance that most fruit have to travel to get to the marketplace. Refrigerating fruit is not the solution as this dulls its flavour, removing the scent and thus a key indicator of ripeness. Nonetheless, all fruit destined for the supermarket will be refrigerated. For this reason I advocate buying locally as often as possible, particularly from farmers' markets if you have one nearby, as this way you can buy directly from the grower, who in turn can hopefully be encouraged to pick ripe and sell immediately, without relying on refrigeration and distant markets. However, I know that this approach is not always possible for everyone.

What to buy in spring

Fruit

- cumquats
- kiwifruit
- loquats
- raspberries (first flush)
- rhubarb (best of all)
- strawberries

Vegetables and herbs

- artichokes
- asparagus
- avocados, hass (at their best from September to January)
- beetroot (continuing into summer too)
- borage
- broad (fava) beans (late ones)
- French tarragon
- garlic (green in September and dried in November)
- jerusalem artichokes
- peas
- potatoes
- rosemary
- sage
- thyme

What to buy in summer

Fruit

- apples (early ones)
- apricots
- avocados, reids (my favourite avocado is at its best from December to January in the Barossa)
- blackberries
- blueberries (continuing into autumn)
- cherries
- fresh currants
- figs (early ones)
- gooseberries
- mangoes
- mulberries (for a short time in January and February in the Barossa)
- nectarines
- passionfruit
- peaches
- pineapples
- plums
- raspberries
- rockmelon
- watermelon

Vegetables and herbs

- basil
- capsicums (peppers) [early ones]
- carrots (at their peak)
- coriander
- cucumbers
- dill
- eggplants (aubergines) [early ones]
- flat beans
- flat-leaf parsley
- lettuces
- potatoes (pink eyes in December and nicolas in February)
- rocket
- sorrel
- squash
- sugar snap peas
- sweet corn
- tomatoes (early ones)
- zucchini (courgettes)

What to buy in autumn

Fruit and nuts

- almonds
- apples (from March new-season golden delicious, galas and, in an early year, fujis; then from May granny smiths, pink ladies and lady williams)
- bananas
- chestnuts
- crabapples
- figs
- grapes
- hazelnuts
- lemons, meyer (in May)
- macadamias (from March to April in the Barossa)
- medlars
- olives
- pears
- persimmons
- pistachios
- pomegranates
- quinces
- walnuts

Vegetables

- broccoli, romanesco
- capsicums (peppers) [at their peak]
- cardoons (early ones)
- chervil
- eggplants (aubergines) [at their peak]
- fennel bulbs (early ones)
- jerusalem artichokes
- lamb's lettuce (mâche)
- mushrooms (wild ones such as saffron milk caps, boletus and pine mushrooms)
- potatoes (kipflers)
- pumpkins (at their peak)
- radicchio
- salsify
- silverbeet and chard
- spinach
- tomatoes (at their peak)
- white sweet potatoes (and continuing into winter)

What to buy
in winter

Fruit and nuts

- chestnuts (in Tasmania late ones arrive in June)
- grapefruit, ruby (brief season from June to July)
- lemons (start in late winter and run from August to November)
- limes (start early in March and continue to July)
- oranges, blood (short season from July to September)
- oranges, navel
- oranges, seville (brief season from July to August)

Vegetables

- avocados, fuerte (at their best from June to October)
- broccolini
- brussels sprouts
- cabbage
- cardoons
- cauliflower
- cavolo nero
- celeriac
- fennel bulbs
- jerusalem artichokes
- kale
- leeks
- onions
- parsnips
- radicchio di Treviso
- rapini
- salsify
- swedes
- sweet potato
- turnips

My basic
kitchen garden

Trees

- bay tree
- lemon tree
  If you have space, and depending on your climate I would include:
- quince tree
- bitter almond tree
- nectarine tree
- apricot tree
- peach tree
- apple tree
- pear tree
- morello cherry tree

Herb garden:

- basil
- flat-leaf parsley
- French tarragon
- garlic
- rosemary
- sage
- thyme
  Where Possible:
- chervil
- coriander
- lavender
- lemon verbena
- sorrel

Buying fish
and seafood

To select fresh fish and seafood use the following guidelines:

- fresh fish smells clean like the sea or even sweet but actually not at all fishy
- the eyes should be bright and clear and the flesh firm
- the colour and vividness of the skin indicate freshness; dry skin indicates age or bad handling
- crustaceans should look bright and have no ammonia smell
- buy seafood on the day you will cook it and make sure you keep it chilled on the journey home
- if you have to refrigerate seafood before cooking, put it in the coldest part of the fridge
- once you get your carefully selected fish or seafood home, take care not to overcook it – it's such a waste!

Once you have your kitchen equipment and larder ingredients to hand and know which fruit, vegetables, herbs and nuts are best to buy each season, there are a few general cooking tips I'd love to share with you. Cooking is made easier when you have bench space around you – when I cook for any more people than just Colin and me, I clear away any clutter so I have as much bench space at my disposal as possible. And I do think it helps to create a pleasant atmosphere, so the next thing is to open as many windows as you can, and, if cooking during the day, let in the natural light. Then there is the issue of music – for me it's either classical or jazz, played very loudly when I'm alone in the kitchen. I'm happy to temper this a little if I am accompanied by a willing helper who has a glass of wine ready for me – and having someone to help with the clean-up rounds off the whole experience!

Some of my key essential ingredients and cooking tips

There is no reason not to have something beautiful to eat at every meal, every day. This doesn't mean being a slave to the kitchen or having to spend a fortune; it is all about understanding the things that will make cooking easier, knowing what questions to ask of your providores and what to look for when shopping for ingredients. I hope that the following tips on ingredients I love and techniques I use all the time will help you to achieve success in your kitchen.

My Four Rules for Fail-safe Results

1. Find the freshest and best possible produce to cook, and treat it with care
2. Keep it simple, especially when cooking for friends - don't become hooked on showing off for dinner parties
3. Get all the ingredients out before you start (if you are really keen, you could even measure them first)
4. Have the right tools and equipment to hand

Anchovies

I love anchovies and tend to use them more than most. Therefore I recommend buying the small 45 gram tins and opening and draining one fresh each time, as anchovies oxidise and turn grey after opening. Even so, there are still times when I have leftover anchovies and as I don't like to store them I recommend mashing the leftovers into some softened butter, along with a squeeze of lemon juice and a grinding of black pepper. Roll the whole lot into a log, wrap it tightly in plastic film and freeze it, with the date and label duly noted on the wrapping. You then have anchovy butter on hand for melting over a piece of perfectly grilled lamb, steak or fish.

Blind baking pastry

Blind baking pastry, that is initially baking an unfilled pastry case at a high temperature before adding the filling, achieves a much better result, in terms of flavour and preventing sogginess.

To blind bake, wrap rolled-out pastry around a rolling pin, then gently unroll it over a tart tin, pressing the pastry into the base and side of the tin. I happily leave the overhanging pastry on at this stage to allow for the shrinkage that usually occurs with pastries such as my Sour-cream Pastry (see recipe page 92). Prick the base of the pastry case with a fork, then chill in the refrigerator for 20 minutes or freezer for 10 minutes; this also helps to prevent shrinkage. Line the pastry case with foil and cover with pastry weights or dried beans (cool and store them in a jar to use when next blind baking); this keeps the foil in place and prevents the pastry from bubbling up as it cooks. Bake in a preheated 200°C (400°F) fan-forced oven for 12–15 minutes. Remove beans and foil and return the pastry case to the oven for another 5–10 minutes or until the base is coloured. The filling should be at an equivalent temperature to the pastry case, so if the filling is at room temperature, then cool the pastry case before filling.

Butter

I always use unsalted butter because I prefer its flavour; I find salted butter too salty and prefer to add salt flakes to a dish myself when I think it needs them. However, unsalted butter does have a shorter shelf-life than the salted variety, which is why I keep it in the freezer until I need it. Often my cooking calls for 'nut-brown' butter, especially when pan-frying or making sauces such as hollandaise and beurre blanc. For this, put butter into a hot pan, then as it begins to bubble, add a splash of extra virgin olive oil to stop it from burning. Keep the pan on the hotplate until the butter turns a deep golden-brown colour and has a 'nutty' flavour.

Caramelised garlic

Whilst garlic cloves can be caramelised on the stove-top I find it easiest to caramelise them in the oven. I choose the smallest pan possible so the garlic fits snugly in one layer (this limits the amount of oil required for cooking), then cover it with olive oil, cook it in a 180°C (350°F) fan-forced oven until the garlic is golden, watching it closely so it doesn't burn.

Chicken – roasting

For me, knowing how to roast a good chook is one of the cornerstones of enjoying a good food life. For my favourite way of doing this, see the recipe for Roast Barossa Chook with Preserved Lemon and Tarragon Butter on page 109.

Chocolate – dark couverture

I only ever use dark couverture chocolate for cooking – look for one with around 70 per cent cocoa solids as the higher the percentage of cocoa solids, the better the result will be.

Citrus fruit

I love using the zest of all citrus fruit, which is why I find a sharp citrus zester an essential tool in my kitchen. When a large quantity of finely grated zest is called for I use a Microplane grater instead, as it gets the job done more quickly. In many of my dishes I use wide strips of

citrus peel, which I remove with a potato peeler and a light hand so that none of the bitter white pith is attached. The key to zesting citrus fruit is to do it at the last moment for maximum flavour.

Cooking times

Don't be too literal with a recipe as there are so many variables at play, starting with the efficiency of your oven, the type of oven used (fan-forced, fan-assisted or conventional); the thickness of a piece of meat, fish or poultry (regardless of its weight) as well as how it was reared; and the age and freshness of the vegetables used that can all affect the final result. Due to all of these factors, it is impossible to provide exact cooking times, down to the last minute. However, for less-experienced cooks, I like to give guidelines for when to check if a dish is ready, as well as a description of what to look for. This brings me to the importance of smelling, feeling and tasting food as you cook; use your instincts and commonsense to guide you and, most importantly, have fun in the process.

Custard as the base for ice cream

If you want to make your own ice cream, you'll need to master the art of making custard. It is important that the egg yolks and sugar are whisked until the mixture is very thick and pale to be sure that the sugar has completely dissolved; this prevents a grainy custard. Cook the custard in a heavy-based saucepan over low–medium heat, stirring continuously until it thickens enough to coat the back of a wooden spoon. If you are concerned about the mixture overheating and curdling, you can cook the custard over a double boiler instead and just accept that this will take longer. To allay any fears of the custard splitting or scrambling if you don't make it often, have a bowl of iced water ready to place the pan in as this reduces the heat, enabling the custard to be rescued (this was a trick I used when I first started making large quantities of custard or crème anglaise). Otherwise, try adding a splash of cold pouring cream to the mixture immediately to impede the cooking process.

For more details on how to make your own ice cream, see the recipe for Passionfruit Parfait on page 200.

Eggplants (Aubergines)

To salt or not to salt is the big question here. In essence, these days salting is not necessary to reduce the bitter-ness of eggplants unless you are using larger, older eggplants with very pronounced seeds. However, much of the bitterness is in their skins, so peeling eggplants before cooking them helps too. Some people have a food intolerance to eggplants (after all, they are a member of the deadly nightshade family), but I've often found that they too can enjoy eggplant if it is peeled.

As I choose to buy young eggplants (or pick them fresh from my garden), the only reason I salt them now is so they will absorb less oil when they cook. And when I do salt, I make sure the eggplant is totally dry before cooking it. When I barbecue or char-grill eggplant, I simply brush a modicum of extra virgin olive oil over the surface and cook it quickly over high heat.

Eggs

We keep our own chooks and I feed them a grain diet, supplemented by vegetable and fruit scraps. An egg boiled for breakfast on the day it is laid is a fabulous thing (see page 54 for a guide to cooking the perfect soft-boiled egg). If I need to supplement my egg supplies, I only ever buy free-range eggs; even then I find their flavour depends on the feed they are given.

Always store your eggs in the refrigerator. As their shells are porous they should be stored pointy-ends down in the carton to minimise their absorption of fridge smells.

You can tell how old an egg is by the structure of the egg white: when fresh the white is viscous, becoming runny and watery as the eggs get older. Fresh eggs are best for poaching as they hold their shape better, while eggs that are a few days old are best for hard-boiling as they are easier to peel. To test whether your eggs are fresh, float them in a bowl of cold water – any that bob to the surface will be off. Fresh eggs will sit at the bottom, while slightly older ones will remain submerged but upright.

When separating yolks and whites it is critical that the yolks are not broken and that no pieces of shell drop into the whites. I suggest first breaking each egg white into a small dish or cup, then transferring the whites and yolks to separate dishes.

Unused egg whites freeze well for up to three months, so if I'm making a yolk-hungry mayonnaise, pasta dough or ice cream I freeze the remaining whites clearly labelled with the number and weight of the whites, as well as the date of freezing.

Older eggs are also better for a recipe requiring whisked egg whites as they will give more volume; this is especially important when making meringues (see recipe for Lime and Coffee Meringues on page 226) and pavlova (see recipe for Chocolate Vino Cotto Pavlova on page 222). It is important that you use room-temperature egg whites for meringues, so remove the eggs from the refrigerator 30 minutes beforehand. Any grease or moisture will stop you in your tracks and ensure failure, so make sure you use a fastidiously clean and dry glass, ceramic or stainless steel bowl and whisk or beaters for maximum volume. Whisk the egg whites continuously, then use them immediately. Take care not to under-whisk or they will not hold their shape. Over-whisking on the other hand gives a dry, granular meringue that will leak moisture. When folding whisked egg whites into a cake mixture, I've learnt to fold in a couple of spoonfuls with a large metal spoon gently before folding in the rest – use an exaggerated motion to fold for the best (that is, lightest) result.

Extra virgin olive oil

My first tip for choosing a good olive oil is to make sure that the date of harvest (not bottling) is clearly stated on the label, as the younger the oil, the better it will be. Extra virgin olive oil is never better than when it has just been crushed, which, in the Barossa, is in early May. It does not 'settle' enough to bottle until August or early September, but producers can store the bulk oil and bottle it at any time during the year.

The test of a good extra virgin olive oil is its freshness on both the nose and palate; after all, it is the juice of the olive and should smell as such. There should not be any sign of rancidity (think of the smell of uncovered butter left at the back of the fridge, or of dirty socks). Everyone has their own flavour preference, so after these vital criteria are met allow personal taste to take over. The key to a good olive oil lies in the balance of freshness of aroma, acidity and pungency – a bland oil is not my style!

Freekeh

I love the nutty flavour of freekeh, or roasted cracked green wheat, and sometimes serve it as a change from other grains such as rice or couscous. To cook enough freekeh for 6–8 people, put 400 g freekeh into a large heavy-based saucepan, then cover with 1.5 litres water

and add 1 tablespoon sea salt. Bring slowly to the boil over low heat, stirring occasionally. When the water is boiling, cover the pan with a tight-fitting lid, then reduce the temperature to low and cook for 10–15 minutes; the freekeh should still be slightly crunchy when cooked. Drain the freekeh, then serve as an accompaniment to the Beef Tagine with Dried Fruit on page 147 or the Pot-roasted Lamb Shoulder with Green Olives, Almonds and Apricots on page 164.

Gelatine leaves

The huge variation in weights, qualities and blooms (that is, setting ability) of gelatine leaves is a particularly vexed issue. All of this is further complicated by the fact that gelatine leaves are generally sold with minimal information. Even so I still prefer to use gelatine leaves instead of gelatine powder as they give a superior result.

My accurate commercial scales tell me that each leaf I buy weighs 2 grams, but this tells me nothing about their bloom or strengths, which can vary considerably. I recommend buying gelatine leaves from a retailer who can provide information on the setting capabilities of their particular products, if possible. Specialty food stores such as Simon Johnson and The Essential Ingredient sell 2 gram gelatine leaves in small packets labelled as 'titanium' or 'gold', a reference to their bloom or strength. Titanium-strength leaves have a stronger setting ability than gold-strength. The set achieved will also depend on the ingredients you are trying to set. Verjuice, for example, is a mild acidulant so more gelatine is needed to set a mixture containing verjuice than would be required for a comparable volume of another mixture containing dairy products or alcohol.

It is vital to soak gelatine leaves in cold water to soften them before adding them to whatever liquid you use – which needs to be just warm enough to dissolve the gelatine but not too hot to render it ineffective.

Meat – cooking

When cooking meat, my first choice for achieving maximum flavour is to cook it on the bone. I realise this may not always be practical when making pies and stews, but I still prefer to cut the meat for these dishes myself. Pre-cut meat loses so much freshness as the cut surfaces are exposed to the air. However, if you have a good butcher, and you are buying the meat just before you want to cook it, by all means have them do it for you.

In temperate climates, meat (and poultry) should be taken out of the refrigerator between 30 minutes and 2 hours before cooking, depending on its size and weight, to allow it to come to room temperature first. Of course, in warmer parts of the country such as the

tropics, not to mention during heatwaves elsewhere, room temperature may exceed safe limits for raw meat, so always err on the side of caution, especially when dealing with poultry.

All meat and poultry needs to be rested after cooking; as a rule of thumb, if it's been cooked quickly, then rest it for a period equivalent to its cooking time. A roast or slow-cooked meat dish should rest for 30 minutes to maximise tenderness by allowing the juices to settle in the meat; you will be surprised by how long a large piece of meat or bird will keep its heat.

Slow-cooking methods, such as braising and stewing, require cuts of meat that retain their shape whilst staying moist during the long cooking period, whereas pan-frying and roasting require prime cuts. For information on specific cuts of meat to suit the different cooking methods, see the meat-based recipes in the 'Middle' chapter (pages 89–179).

Nuts and nut oils

I generally store shelled almonds, hazelnuts, macadamias, pine nuts and walnuts in the refrigerator as they are very prone to rancidity. I suggest storing large quantities of these nuts in the freezer. I also keep opened bottles of nut oils in the refrigerator as, unlike extra virgin olive oil, they don't solidify when chilled and last for a fair while if well sealed.

In all my recipes calling for nuts I roast the nuts first to maximise their flavour. I preheat a fan-forced oven to 180°C (350°F) and roast them until just golden; you will need to keep a close eye on them as they can burn quickly, especially pine nuts. Almonds, hazelnuts and walnuts will take about 10 minutes, although the exact time depends on their freshness and the ferocity (or otherwise) of your oven, so watch them too. Walnuts and hazelnuts need their skins rubbed off after roasting. I generally wrap the hot nuts in a clean tea towel and rub them vigorously; if they are too hot to handle, use thick kitchen gloves. Sift the nuts to remove the skins, then proceed with the recipe.

Pasta

The best-quality dried pastas I have eaten are made by artisanal producers in Italy. It is not just the great flour that makes great pasta, but the bronze dies used to form the pasta shapes. Artisanal producers use textured dies that give a rougher surface to the pasta, meaning the sauce will cling to it more. Modern dies are made from Teflon, which creates a smoother-surfaced pasta that the sauces slide off. Another critical factor is the natural slow-drying process that artisanal producers use; this also adds so much to the texture and therefore quality of the pasta. I always keep a supply of Martelli-brand penne and spaghetti in my larder.

Pastry and pasta-making

It's difficult to provide exact measurements or quantities of binding ingredients to be added to flour, whether it be egg yolks for pasta (see recipe page 76) or sour cream for my Sour-cream Pastry (see recipe page 92), as it depends so much on the quality, makeup and age of the flour, not to mention the weather (on a humid day, less liquid is generally required). I find it best to add three-quarters of the amount suggested in the recipe, then add the rest as required.

Potatoes

After experiencing extraordinary potatoes at Dunan, on Scotland's Isle of Skye, where we pulled seaweed over the crop, resulting in potatoes that were so flavoursome that all they needed was lashings of butter to make a meal in their own right, I must confess to not bothering with what I considered to be rather ordinary potatoes during the fifteen years when I ran the Pheasant Farm restaurant. I never had potatoes on the menu in all that time; such was my lack of interest in them. However, that all changed when waxy varieties became available in Australia. Waxy potatoes, such as pink eyes from Tasmania (also called southern golds), bintjes, kipflers, pink fir apples, desirees (a great all-rounder) and my favourites, nicolas or dutch creams, have the dense, rich texture and buttery flavour that I prefer. Floury potato varieties, such as sebagos, russets, king edwards and kennebecs, are lower in moisture but have a higher starch content. The only time I use them is on the rare occasion when I want to cook chips, when I turn to either king edward or russet burbank potatoes.

Post-cooking marinades or 'baths'

I love to use a post-cooking marinade or 'bath' after barbecuing or char-grilling. The intense searing heat of the barbecue adds great flavour but it can easily dry out the meat. By having a 'bath' of extra virgin olive oil and verjuice, lemon juice or good-quality aged vinegar ready, the hot meat seems to soak up the juices, becoming impregnated with the flavours. I add whatever is in season and to hand to the marinade; in autumn this means grapes, walnuts or fresh figs (see my recipe for Spatchcock in a Fig Bath on page 98), but at other times it might mean loads of fresh herbs and lemon.

Parmigiano Reggiano

Real Parmigiano Reggiano is produced according to time-honoured methods within a designated area of northern Italy. This cheese has a great heritage, and its quality and authenticity are guaranteed by its PDO (Protected Designation of Origin) status. Beyond that, as with many ingredients, there are Parmigianos and then there are Parmigianos, and the quality of their flavour is based both on age and excellence of handling (in Australia, Will Studd of the Calendar Cheese Company and Simon Johnson are the experts in handling imported

cheeses with proper care). Whilst we do produce parmesan-style cheese in Australia, in the main I know of no specialist Australian cheese-maker using traditional methods. The local parmesans I have tasted are made and matured under plastic, which means they will never have the complexity of flavour and wonderful tradition of true PDO-certified Parmigiano Reggiano.

Risotto

I use imported Italian risotto rice, which can be arborio, carnaroli or vialone nano. My favourite of all is the Ferron brand carnaroli rice sold in blue and white bags. I find that a wide, heavy-based, deep-sided frying pan, a good wooden spoon and a ladle for adding the stock are the perfect tools for cooking risotto. See the recipe for Radicchio Risotto on page 118 for more details on how to cook risotto.

Sterilising jars

I only bother to sterilise jars when I'm making a preserve that is to be added to the jar cold. If you are making jam or chutney that is hotter than 80°C (176°F) when the jars are filled, then the mixture will be sufficiently hot to sterilise the jars; just turn the well-sealed jars upside down to sterilise the lids too. However, if you are unsure of the temperature or are cold-filling the jars, then wash the jars thoroughly in hot water with detergent, rinse and leave to drain upside down on a clean tea towel,

taking care to handle only the outside of the jars. Preheat a fan-forced oven to 100°C (212°F) and place the jars and their lids (if they are heatproof) in the oven for 10 minutes. Turn off the heat, then leave the jars to cool in the oven, again taking care to handle only the outsides of the jars.

Stocks

Good homemade stock is an essential part of my cooking. Making a stock should be a labour of love. The quality of each ingredient, from the chook or bones to the vegetables, will make a remarkable difference to the end result. I'd say it is almost impossible to get a commercial stock made with as much care as one you'd make yourself (although I am working on this!).

To make my Golden Chicken Stock, place a jointed 2.2 kg boiler or breeder chook (or 3 kg roughly chopped meaty bones), 2 halved, unpeeled onions and 1 roughly chopped carrot in a roasting pan, drizzle with a little extra virgin olive oil, then roast in a fan-forced 200°C (400°F) oven for 20 minutes or until the chicken and the vegetables are golden brown. Transfer the chicken and the vegetables to a large stockpot, then, if you like, deglaze the roasting pan over high heat with 100 ml white wine and add to the stockpot, along with 1 roughly chopped large leek, 1 roughly chopped celery stick, 1 bay leaf, 6 stalks thyme, 6 stalks flat-leaf parsley and 1 head garlic, halved through the middle. Cover with about 2.5 litres water, then simmer uncovered for 3-4 hours. Strain through a sieve into a bowl, then cool quickly by immersing the bowl in a sink of cold water. Refrigerate to let any fat settle on the surface, then remove solidified fat. The stock will keep for 4 days in the refrigerator or 3 months in the freezer - be sure to label and date the container.

Sugar syrup

To make a simple sugar syrup, combine 1 cup caster sugar with 1 cup water in a small saucepan. Slowly bring to the boil over low heat, stirring continuously until sugar dissolves, then leave to cool. Refrigerate and use within 1 week.

Vegetables - cooking

Generally speaking, when cooking vegetables that grow below the ground, such as potatoes, carrots and beetroot, begin cooking them in cold water; tiny new potatoes are the exception to this rule. I generally put vegetables grown above the ground - like beans, peas, broad (fava) beans and brussels sprouts - straight into a pan of boiling water. I don't refresh vegetables in iced water to stop them cooking further. Instead I judge the

cooking time carefully, then drain and drizzle them with extra virgin olive oil or add a little butter to melt over them whilst they are still hot – I'm not concerned if they lose a bit of heat in the process.

Vinaigrette

The ratio of oil to acidulant (be it verjuice, lemon juice, wine vinegar or vino cotto) will vary depending not only on whether the oil you use is extra virgin olive oil or a nut oil, but on the individual tastes of the cook. As a basic rule of thumb for a vinaigrette, I use four parts extra virgin olive oil to one part good-quality aged red-wine vinegar. However, if I'm making a walnut oil and verjuice vinaigrette I will use almost equal quantities of both. I also add sea salt and freshly ground black pepper and often a little Dijon mustard. Other options include adding a splash of pouring cream to soften the vinaigrette, or finely chopped golden shallots, finely grated citrus zest, almost any fresh herb, and, depending on your tastes, a sprinkle of caster sugar.

Water Bath

I use a water bath (also called a bain marie) when I'm cooking something fragile like a crème caramel or the Baked Vanilla Custard with Coffee Jelly on page 188, where it's important that it sets all over at the same time, or something like a pâté or terrine, which needs to cook through evenly while remaining moist (see the recipe for Pumpkin, Walnut, Cheese and Verjuice Terrine on page 44). To cook with a water bath, choose a sturdy heatproof container that will accommodate the mould/s, then place the mould/s inside it. Pour enough hot water from the kettle into the container (a roasting pan is good) to come to about four-fifths of the way up the sides of the mould/s (follow the instructions in individual recipes – sometimes you may only need to fill the water bath to come halfway up the sides of the moulds), then carefully place the container into a preheated oven. Alternatively, if you are at all concerned about the safety of transferring the water-filled container to the oven, you can place the container with the moulds into the oven, then add the boiling water. If you have a steam oven you can dispense with the need for a water bath.

Beginning

Mozzarella Sandwiches

200 g buffalo mozzarella or bocconcini,
cut into 1 cm thick slices

1 teaspoon finely grated lemon zest

squeeze of lemon juice

extra virgin olive oil, for drizzling

sea salt and freshly ground black pepper

8 slices pancetta, cut into strips

4 slices day-old white bread,
crusts trimmed

50 g unsalted butter, softened

4–6 basil leaves, torn

SERVES 2 AS A LIGHT SUPPER

Colin loves to make toasted cheese sandwiches for Sunday night tea on those occasions when we've had a long lunch and don't really need anything else. But I must confess that often we end up both feeling just hungry enough to succumb to raiding the refrigerator, and, if I leave it up to Colin, I know what we eat will be very basic.

Then one weekend, when we knew friends were coming to stay, the thought of Sunday night supper toasties led me to buy fresh mozzarella to be the hero of the sandwiches, rather than them just being a product of leftovers. These sandwiches are very more-ish – and, yes, they are made with ordinary white bread. You could also use a sandwich maker for toasting them, if you've got one.

- Marinate cheese with lemon zest and juice, a splash of olive oil and a little salt and pepper for 1 hour.
- Cook pancetta in a dry frying pan over medium heat until crisp, then set aside to drain on paper towel.
- Flatten bread with a rolling pin, then butter each slice sparingly. Place 2 of the slices, buttered-sides down, on a chopping board and divide the marinated mozzarella between them. Add torn basil, season with salt to taste and crumble on the crisp pancetta. Top with remaining slices of bread, buttered-sides up, then gently fry in a heavy-based frying pan over medium heat until golden on both sides. Use your fingers to put any pieces that fall out back in; these are generous sandwiches.
- Remove sandwiches from the pan and serve.

Salad of Beetroot, Blood Orange and Pumpkin

1 bunch baby beetroot, leaves trimmed leaving 2 cm stalks attached (this prevents them from 'bleeding' into the water)

sea salt

2 tablespoons red-wine vinegar

extra virgin olive oil, for drizzling

470 g jap or Queensland blue pumpkin, seeded and cut into 3 × 3.5 cm wedges

¼ cup sage leaves

60 g unsalted butter, chopped

sea salt

2 blood oranges, thinly sliced widthways

1 tablespoon chopped chives

1 bunch watercress, sprigs picked

1 head witlof (optional), outer leaves discarded and inner leaves separated

VINAIGRETTE

1 tablespoon honey

¼ cup extra virgin olive oil

2 tablespoons red-wine vinegar

sea salt and freshly ground black pepper

SERVES 6 AS AN ACCOMPANIMENT OR 3 AS A LIGHT LUNCHEON DISH

I can find a million ways to bring roast pumpkin into my diet – it's finding a good pumpkin that's the hard part. I'm always on the look-out, so when I see a great pumpkin (freshly cut, of course to show depth of colour and ripeness) I take it home to cook with whatever else is in season. Autumn is absolutely the best time for pumpkins, although they are grown year-round in warmer climes.

I've also used beetroot, another of my favourites. No matter how many times I boil or roast beetroot, it always surprises me just how long it takes them to cook; even so this is a dish where I'd always go to the trouble of cooking them from scratch. Whilst I admit to having sliced tinned beetroot in the pantry for hamburgers or steak sandwiches (see recipe page 150), the acidity of canned baby beets won't add to this dish. I've used blood oranges too – their amazing colour and sweet-sour notes complement any dish they are added to.

- Bring beetroot to the boil in a saucepan of salted water with 1 tablespoon of the vinegar added. Reduce heat to low and cook for 50 minutes or until tender. To test whether they are cooked, insert a sharp knife into the largest beetroot; if it inserts easily the beetroot are ready. Drain beetroot and place in a bowl of cold water, then leave to cool slightly before slipping the skins off by hand; it's easier to do this while they are still a little warm. Cut into quarters, drizzle with remaining red-wine vinegar and a splash of olive oil, then sprinkle with salt and set aside.

- Preheat fan-forced oven to 200ºC (400ºF).

- Meanwhile, cut pumpkin wedges in half widthways, then place on a baking tray, drizzle with olive oil, sprinkle with salt and roast for about 20 minutes or until cooked and coloured but still firm. Leave to cool, then peel.

- Place sage leaves on a baking tray and dot with small pieces of butter. Bake for about 8 minutes or until butter starts to sizzle and sage leaves are crisp; take care as they burn easily.

- Mix beetroot, pumpkin, blood orange slices, chives, watercress and witlof, if using, in a serving bowl.

- For the vinaigrette, combine all the ingredients in a small bowl and season to taste.

- Add enough dressing to salad to just coat, then toss to combine. Scatter with the crisp sage leaves and serve.

Heritage Tomato Salad

700 g assorted heritage tomatoes, larger ones cut into 2 cm thick slices and smaller ones halved lengthways

¼ cup firmly-packed basil leaves

¼ cup flat-leaf parsley leaves

1 heaped tablespoon chopped oregano

a handful of rocket leaves

1 small red onion, thinly sliced

extra virgin olive oil, for drizzling

vino cotto or balsamic vinegar, for drizzling

sea salt and freshly ground black pepper

2 heaped tablespoons gruth (soft, fresh cheese made in the Barossa) or other soft cow's milk cheese

SERVES 4 AS AN ACCOMPANIMENT

This salad came into being when I was given about thirty different varieties of ripe heritage tomatoes, each variety packaged in a labelled paper bag. This thoughtful gift provided me with enough of each variety of tomato to taste and work out my favourites (plus decide which ones to plant in my garden), as well as enough to make a beautiful salad of differing shapes, colours and sizes. The winners were the green zebra, black krim and rouge de marmande varieties.

- Place tomatoes, herbs, rocket and onion in a mixing bowl, then add a drizzle of olive oil and a good splash of vino cotto and season to taste with salt and pepper. Mix well, then transfer to a serving dish. Top with gruth and drizzle with a little more olive oil, then serve.

Spaghetti with Crab

12 cloves garlic

sea salt

extra virgin olive oil, for cooking and drizzling

100 g snow peas (mange-touts), thinly sliced

¼ bulb fennel (including fronds), thinly sliced

¼ cup lemon juice, plus extra for coating

200 g top-quality dried spaghetti

⅔ cup mascarpone

finely grated zest of 2 lemons

freshly ground black pepper

120 g freshly cooked and picked crab meat (3-4 cooked blue swimmer crabs)

chervil leaves, to serve

SERVES 4 AS AN ENTRÉE

Once again, the success of this dish relies on starting with a good larder. Using a really top-quality artisanal pasta, usually from Italy, makes all the difference, as such a pasta is so flavoursome in its own right that all it needs is some extra virgin olive oil, garlic and perhaps some Parmigiano Reggiano to make a delicious meal. Then, when you add a little freshly caught, cooked and picked blue swimmer crab meat, you've got a meal worthy of the most fastidious guests at your table. I must emphasise the importance of using freshly caught and cooked crabs; once you have access to these you'll never want to eat blue swimmer crabs any other way again. The snow peas can be replaced with freshly podded peas, if you can get them.

- Blanch garlic cloves in a small saucepan of boiling salted water for 5 minutes, then drain and peel. Heat 1 tablespoon olive oil in a frying pan over low heat, then sauté garlic for 7 minutes or until golden and almost cooked through. Remove and set aside.
- Blanch snow peas in the same pan, then drain and thinly slice.
- Toss fennel in a little of the lemon juice to prevent it from browning and set aside.
- Cook spaghetti in a large saucepan of boiling salted water following manufacturers' instructions, then drain.
- Melt mascarpone in a large frying pan over low heat. Add remaining lemon juice and zest, then season with pepper and add caramelised garlic and snow peas and stir to combine. Toss in cooked (not rinsed) pasta, then increase the heat to high to heat through before adding the crab. Remove from the heat and toss the crab through the pasta, then add the fennel.
- Divide pasta between 4 plates, then top with chervil leaves, add a final drizzle of olive oil and serve.

Cauliflower with Toasted Crumbs

1 small head cauliflower, cut into
2 cm florets

1 head garlic, cloves separated

⅓ cup extra virgin olive oil

2 tablespoons lemon thyme leaves

1½ cups coarse sourdough breadcrumbs
(made from about ½ loaf)

1 × 45 g tin anchovies, drained

2 tablespoons coarsely chopped
flat-leaf parsley

¼ cup grated pecorino, to serve

SERVES 4 AS AN ACCOMPANIMENT
OR ENTRÉE

If the mark of being vegetarian was based on a love of vegetables, then I'd be one (I just have trouble leaving out the meat, offal, poultry and fish!). For some reason I've never successfully grown cauliflowers, so luckily I get the chance to buy small heads from our Saturday-morning Barossa Farmers' Markets during winter, which is their season. Cauliflower is a vegetable I enjoy so much that I feel it actually needs nothing more than a drizzle of extra virgin olive oil and a smattering of sea salt and freshly ground black pepper to be utterly delicious. But if you want to serve cauli as a dish in its own right then go the extra mile, as I've done here, by adding the crunch of breadcrumbs and the pungent saltiness of anchovies.

• Blanch cauliflower in a saucepan of boiling salted water, then remove with a slotted spoon. Blanch garlic cloves in the same pan for 5 minutes, then drain and peel.

• Heat 1 tablespoon of the olive oil in a frying pan over low heat, then sauté garlic for 7 minutes or until golden and almost cooked through. Remove and set aside. Add remaining olive oil, lemon thyme and cauliflower florets to the pan and cook over medium heat for 4–5 minutes or until cauliflower is golden and cooked through. Add breadcrumbs and cook, stirring until golden and crisp, then add anchovies, parsley and garlic and stir to combine.

• Add grated pecorino, then serve.

Cavolo Nero

1 bunch (about 700 g) cavolo nero, washed and chopped

50 g unsalted butter

1 tablespoon extra virgin olive oil

2 small golden shallots, thinly sliced

½ quince, peeled, cored and coarsely grated

½ teaspoon lemon juice

SERVES 4 AS AN ACCOMPANIMENT

I am happy to feel at least a little responsible for being part of the push to encourage the growing of this great vegetable in Australia. Left in the ground to mature it becomes a majestic plant indeed. I enjoy the baby leaves in autumn salads. However, the slightly larger leaves, which I pick after the frosts have hit a little later in the year, have the best flavour of all and I use them in minestrone or cooked as a vegetable accompaniment, liberally doused with robust new-season extra virgin olive oil. If you can't find quinces they can be substituted with beurre bosc pears, to great effect.

- Blanch cavolo nero in a saucepan of boiling water for 3 minutes or until just tender; how long it takes depends on the age of the cabbage. Drain well and squeeze out any excess moisture.
- Heat butter in a large frying pan over medium heat until nut-brown, then add olive oil to inhibit burning. Add shallots and quince and cook until tender and golden.
- Add lemon juice, and cavolo nero, then toss to combine and serve.

Orecchiette with Rapini, Broccolini, Cauliflower and Pecorino

⅔ cup coarse breadcrumbs

extra virgin olive oil, for cooking

100 g orecchiette

sea salt

1 bunch broccolini, trimmed and cut into 5 cm lengths

150 g cauliflower florets

10 leaves rapini (optional), also known as cimi di rapa (I added them simply because I had some growing in my garden)

4 cloves garlic, finely chopped

1 × 45 g tin anchovies, drained (optional)

⅓ cup flat-leaf parsley, roughly chopped

⅓ cup shaved pecorino, to serve

SERVES 4 AS AN ENTRÉE

Having a stockpile of good-quality dried pasta in a range of shapes is a must in my larder. As well as Italian pasta made from hard durum wheat flour, I also stock spelt pasta made by artisanal producers in Italy, for those who find durum wheat flour hard to digest. I am on the look-out for Australian pasta producers who are driven by the principles of great flavour and who hand-make and slow-dry their pasta. It seems to me that only the older artisanal companies use traditional bronze casts rather than the modern Teflon-coated ones, giving the pasta more texture, which means the sauce adheres to it more.

This is one of those dishes that can be made in the time it takes for the pasta to cook, so it could almost be called 'fast food'. In simple dishes such as this, once again it's the quality of each ingredient that allows the end result to shine.

- Preheat fan-forced oven to 200°C (400°F).
- Place breadcrumbs on a baking tray, drizzle with olive oil and bake for 8 minutes or until crisp and golden. Leave to cool.
- Cook orecchiette in a large saucepan of boiling salted water following the manufacturer's instructions.
- Meanwhile, working in batches, blanch broccolini, then cauliflower, then rapini, if using, in another saucepan of boiling salted water for 2–3 minutes or until tender, then drain and set aside.
- Heat ⅓ cup olive oil in a frying pan over medium heat, then add garlic and cook gently for 5 minutes or until golden. Add broccolini, cauliflower and rapini, if using, to pan and toss to combine. Toss in breadcrumbs, anchovies, if using, and drained (but not rinsed) orecchiette and heat through, adding a splash more olive oil to moisten.
- Season to taste with salt, then serve topped with parsley and shaved pecorino.

Pumpkin, Walnut, Cheese and Verjuice Terrine

150 g walnuts

750 g really ripe peeled, seeded and cubed pumpkin pieces

2 tablespoons extra virgin olive oil, plus extra for drizzling

1 tablespoon finely chopped lemon thyme

sea salt and freshly ground black pepper

⅓ cup verjuice

150 g fresh ricotta

150 g white Castello cheese

2 tablespoons sage, finely chopped

¼ teaspoon ground nutmeg

6 free-range eggs

8-10 vine leaves (either blanched fresh vine leaves or preserved in brine and well rinsed)

walnut oil (optional), for drizzling

lamb's lettuce (mâche) or rocket (optional), to serve

SERVES 8-10 AS A LUNCHEON DISH

It is only worth entertaining the idea of making this dish if you've found a wonderfully ripe, deep-coloured pumpkin, the star ingredient here. It makes a great luncheon dish for guests as all the work is done the day before and it really gets a chance to set in the terrine mould in the refrigerator overnight. Make sure that it's really cold before cutting it, and use a serrated knife to cut through the vine leaves. Add a spoonful or two of Eggplant Pickle (see recipe page 74) as an accompaniment if you want to serve it as a main meal.

◆ Preheat fan-forced oven to 180°C (350°F).

◆ Place walnuts on a baking tray and bake for 10 minutes, checking frequently to make sure they don't burn. Immediately wrap with a clean tea towel, then rub to peel off skins. Sift rubbed walnuts through a sieve to get rid of skins, then leave to cool. Roughly chop cooled walnuts and set aside.

◆ Increase oven temperature to 200°C (400°F).

◆ Place pumpkin, the olive oil, thyme and a little salt and pepper on a baking tray, tossing until well combined. Roast pumpkin for 30 minutes or until soft and caramelised. Deglaze pan with verjuice and return to the oven for 5 minutes or until verjuice has completely evaporated. Leave to cool. Reduce oven temperature to 180°C (350°F).

◆ Meanwhile, mix ricotta, Castello, sage and nutmeg with the lightly beaten white of one of the eggs until well combined.

◆ Place cooled roast pumpkin, eggs and remaining egg yolk in a food processor and process until well combined.

◆ Lightly grease a 12 × 22 × 6.5 cm loaf tin, then line base and sides with vine leaves, reserving 1 or 2 leaves for later use.

◆ Scatter walnuts over base of the prepared loaf tin. Spoon cheese mixture over the walnuts, then pour over pumpkin mixture and cover with remaining vine leaves. Transfer loaf tin to a deep roasting pan, then pour in enough boiling water to come about halfway up the sides of the loaf tin.

◆ Bake for 30 minutes or until pumpkin mixture is set; a skewer inserted into the centre should come out clean. Remove water bath from oven and leave terrine to cool in the water bath. Remove tin from water bath, then cover tin with plastic film and refrigerate overnight.

◆ Cut thick slices of the terrine, then drizzle with olive oil or walnut oil, if using, and season with salt and pepper. Serve with mâche or rocket to the side.

Globe Artichokes with Pastry and Preserved Lemon

6 globe artichokes

⅓ cup verjuice or lemon juice

⅓ cup extra virgin olive oil

sea salt

3 sheets filo pastry, each cut into four 15 cm rounds

120 g soft goat's cheese

freshly ground black pepper

flat-leaf parsley leaves, to serve

PRESERVED LEMON BUTTER

100 g unsalted butter, chopped and softened

1 tablespoon rinsed and finely chopped preserved lemon rind

SERVES 4 AS AN ENTRÉE

Over the years I've had so many wonderful meals with my friend Stephanie Alexander, from the halcyon days of her eponymous restaurant, through to her time at the Richmond Hill Café and Larder, where every once in a while we would cook a special dinner together. At one of these dinners, Stephanie presented a dish similar to these little tarts as one of her courses. What I really loved about them was the idea of using *brik*, the thin Tunisian pastry, as it was just perfect for making entrée-sized serves. As *brik* isn't readily available in Adelaide, I've used filo here instead. The preserved lemon butter is in keeping with the North African origins of the *brik* pastry originally used.

◆ For the preserved lemon butter, combine butter and preserved lemon, then set aside.

◆ Trim and discard the top third of the artichokes, then pull off the outer leaves and discard. Use a teaspoon to scoop out the hairy chokes, then trim the bases of the stems with a small sharp knife and cut each artichoke in half lengthways. Put the prepared artichokes immediately in the verjuice or a bowl of water acidulated with lemon juice to prevent browning.

◆ Pat artichokes dry with paper towels. Heat olive oil in a stainless steel frying pan over low-medium heat, then slowly fry artichokes, with a little salt added, turning them frequently, until golden on the outside and meltingly tender on the inside; this can take up to 15 minutes, depending on their size, variety and age. Take care that the oil does not become too hot, as the exteriors will burn before the interiors cook. Place on paper towels to drain excess oil.

◆ Preheat fan-forced oven to 220°C (450°F).

◆ Gently soften the preserved lemon butter so that it spreads easily. Place 4 filo rounds on a baking tray lined with baking paper, then brush each generously with melted preserved lemon butter, and top with another pastry round. Brush with more of the melted butter and top with remaining pastry rounds, then brush with butter again. Bake for 4-5 minutes or until pastry just starts to brown.

◆ Remove pastry rounds from oven, top each with 1½ artichoke hearts and one-quarter of the goat's cheese, then pop back into the oven for another 5 minutes.

◆ Season pastries to taste with salt and pepper, then top with flat-leaf parsley leaves, drizzle with olive oil and serve.

Broccoli with Almonds and Lemon Butter

50 g almond flakes

1 head broccoli, cut into florets

100 g unsalted butter, chopped

extra virgin olive oil, for cooking

juice of 1 lemon

sea salt and freshly ground black pepper

SERVES 4 AS AN ACCOMPANIMENT

Now that we have easy access to it, good-quality broccoli seems to have become a staple vegetable on dinner plates these days. Whilst we all know that broccoli is very good for us, even so it can be a bit boring. I must admit to having a preference for broccoli stalks over the heads, but when tossed in a pan with nut-brown butter, almonds and lemon juice, I'll gladly eat every bit of it. This is delicious served alongside the Char-grilled Lamb on page 97.

♦ Preheat fan-forced oven to 180°C (350°F). Place almond flakes on a baking tray and roast for 5 minutes or until golden, then set aside to cool.

♦ Blanch broccoli in a saucepan of boiling salted water.

♦ Meanwhile, melt butter with a splash of olive oil in a frying pan over medium-high heat. Add almond flakes and toss, then drain broccoli and immediately add to the pan. Deglaze pan with lemon juice, then transfer to a serving plate and serve immediately, seasoned with salt and pepper.

Perfect Omelette with Baked Mushrooms

4 medium-sized swiss brown mushrooms

50 g unsalted butter, plus extra for cooking

sea salt and freshly ground black pepper

4 stalks thyme

3 free-range eggs (50 g each)

1 tablespoon pouring cream

2 tablespoons mascarpone

roughly chopped flat-leaf parsley and toasted wholegrain bread, to serve

SERVES 1

Omelette-making used to frighten me – more precisely, how to stop the eggs from scrambling and instead become that wonderfully cohesive dish that a perfect omelette is. Adding a luscious filling just caps it all off – this time I've used mascarpone, but you could use your favourite cheese or fresh herbs, to name just a few options.

The trick is to use a good pan. Whilst I have a traditional black steel omelette pan, which I use for this purpose only, a good small non-stick frying pan will also do a great job. I make sure I always wipe my pan clean after each use rather than washing it, to preserve the surface and not create any rust spots that would act as magnets for an omelette. I also ensure the pan is sufficiently hot that a small piece of butter will sizzle in it without browning. I find a non-stick spatula a great tool, as it is just the thing for dragging through the quickly setting egg to allow the unset centre to flow to the sides of the pan.

The keys to a good omelette really are confidence, practice and speed – no more than ninety seconds in total and it's cooked.

♦ Preheat fan-forced oven to 180°C (350°F).

♦ Lay mushrooms on a baking tray, stem-sides up, then spread one-quarter of the butter evenly over each one. Season to taste with salt and pepper, then top each mushroom with 1 stalk thyme and bake for 10 minutes.

♦ Crack eggs into a bowl and stir very lightly, so the yolks and whites break up a little but are not completely incorporated. Swirl in cream and season to taste with a pinch each of salt and pepper.

♦ Heat a small frying pan over medium heat, then add a knob of butter. Once the butter has melted, increase the heat to medium-high, then pour in the eggs and tip the pan to distribute the egg mixture evenly. Drag a spatula or fork through from sides of pan to middle to pull eggs away from the sides, then cook until most of the mixture is set, but still looks a little runny. Remove from heat. Add mascarpone to centre of the omelette, then tilt the pan and gently fold the omelette in half, encasing the mascarpone; the egg mixture will continue to cook.

♦ Loosen the base of the omelette with a spatula, then slide it onto a warm plate and scatter with chopped parsley. Serve with baked mushrooms and wholegrain toast to the side.

Mozzarella with Crème Fraîche and Figs – My Take on *Burrata*

1 × 500 g ball fresh mozzarella (I use fior di latte), cut into 8 mm thick slices

½ cup crème fraîche

¼ cup full-cream milk

1½ teaspoons finely grated lemon zest

3 teaspoons lemon juice, plus extra to serve

sea salt and freshly ground black pepper

2 tablespoons extra virgin olive oil

6 large ripe figs, cut into 2 mm thick slices

2 tablespoons honey (the more intensely flavoured it is, the better – I like to use leatherwood or manuka)

2 tablespoons thinly sliced basil

2 tablespoons thinly sliced mint

2 tablespoons roughly chopped marjoram

crusty bread, to serve

SERVES 6

The first time I tried *burrata* was in Los Angeles, at the table of famed La Brea Bakery chef, Nancy Silverton. The second time I ate it was in January 2007, also at Nancy's table, this time at her recently opened LA restaurant Pizzeria Mozza. This delicacy really hit me between the eyes, as it embodied everything I love about Italian food. *Burrata* is basically a ball of super-fresh mozzarella (with debate as to whether it was originally made from cow's or buffalo's milk) that is impregnated with cream. It's a specialty of Puglia and is flown into both coasts of the United States each week. We don't get the real thing imported from Italy into Australia, although I've recently discovered the Cairns-based Vannella Cheese Factory makes its own *burrata*, but as yet it isn't widely available. This recipe is my way of approximating the creamy texture and complex sweet flavour I remember from my trip to L.A. At various times I have presented this dish with caramelised onions, eaten it with roasted baby beetroots glazed with vino cotto or served it with roasted tomatoes and pesto. However, this combination with fresh figs is the one I love most.

• Place sliced mozzarella in a single layer in a large, shallow dish. Mix together crème fraîche and milk, blending well to combine, then add lemon zest and juice and mix well again. Pour milk mixture over mozzarella, making sure that each slice is completely coated on both sides. Sprinkle with 1 heaped tablespoon salt and a little pepper, then drizzle generously with olive oil. Cover with plastic film and leave in the refrigerator overnight to marinate, turning mozzarella slices after 12 hours.

• Place sliced figs in a shallow dish and drizzle with honey, making sure that each fig slice has been drizzled. Add a good squeeze of lemon juice, then season to taste.

• Transfer mozzarella slices to a serving plate, then top with the marinated figs. Scatter with herbs, then add a final drizzle of olive oil. Serve with crusty bread.

Oyster Shooters

½ × 2 g gelatine leaf

½ cup verjuice

½ teaspoon caster sugar

6 oysters, freshly shucked

½ golden shallot, finely chopped

1 tablespoon sherry vinegar

½ teaspoon thyme, finely chopped

sea salt and freshly ground black pepper

MAKES 6 SHOOTERS

One year, a great caterer and friend of mine, Cath Kerry, introduced a verjuice oyster shooter to as many of her customers as she possibly could. I thought it a great idea, then, given my love of jellies, took it a step further by adding gelatine. Having the oysters encased in a soft verjuice jelly, with the surprise of the thyme and vinegar on top, is both a taste and textural sensation – and it's so simple to do. And oh what a difference it makes if you shuck your own oysters!

These shooters are best when the jelly is only just softly set so that the jelly-encased oyster slips easily out of its glass.

- Soak gelatine leaf in cold water for a couple of minutes to soften.
- Heat verjuice and sugar in a small saucepan over high heat until sugar dissolves, then leave to cool a little. Squeeze excess liquid out of the gelatine leaf and stir it into lukewarm verjuice until dissolved.
- Divide one-third of the verjuice mixture between 6 shot glasses, then refrigerate until jelly sets. Keep remaining two-thirds in a warm place so that it doesn't set while mixture in glasses is in the refrigerator. If it does start to set, gently reheat over low heat.
- Place a freshly shucked oyster on top of each of the set jellies, then top with the remaining verjuice mixture and refrigerate until set.
- Meanwhile, mix shallot, sherry vinegar and thyme, then season to taste and leave for 20 minutes for flavours to infuse.
- Top each shot glass with a little of the shallot mixture, then serve each one with a teaspoon so that your guests can enjoy their oyster shooter in one go.

Preserved Figs

½ cup raw sugar

½ cup water

¾ cup Stone's Green Ginger Wine

¾ cup verjuice

juice of 1 lemon

1-2 small sticks cinnamon

20 small green figs, halved lengthways

MAKES 1 × 1 LITRE JAR

I make this preserve with the small figs that are left on my tree at the end of their season – they never totally ripen but I can't bear the waste of throwing them out. I had no idea how well figs would preserve in verjuice until one of our fig growers brought me a jar at the end of the season; I could see what a great flavour combination it was. So, at the end of each fig season, I now set out to collect these late figs which even the birds seem to reject, to preserve and serve alongside a terrine, a poached chook breast or even as an accompaniment to a really ripe goat's cheese.

- Place sugar, water, ginger wine and verjuice in a medium-sized saucepan and slowly bring to the boil over low heat, stirring occasionally to dissolve sugar. Once syrup has come to the boil, add lemon juice and cinnamon, then simmer for 5-10 minutes until the syrup has reduced slightly.
- Place halved figs in a sterilised (see page 27) 1-litre capacity jar, then pour hot syrup over and seal immediately. Although there should be enough acidity to store the sealed figs at room temperature, to be absolutely sure they won't spoil, store in the refrigerator.

Cucumber Gazpacho

2 slices day-old sourdough or wood-fired bread, crusts discarded and bread torn

2 tablespoons coconut milk, plus 1 tablespoon extra, to serve

¼ cup water

2 small spring onions

1 small clove garlic, crushed

⅓ cup extra virgin olive oil

2 large telegraph cucumbers, peeled and roughly chopped

¾ cup verjuice

sea salt and freshly ground black pepper

small mint leaves, to serve

SERVES 4

This is a refreshing summer soup, best made the day before serving so that it has the chance to really chill in the refrigerator. The addition of coconut milk acts as a high note to complement the cucumber. For the best results, don't stint on the quality of the bread, and don't over-soak it either.

- Place bread in a bowl. Combine coconut milk with water, then pour mixture over bread and leave to soften, but don't let it become soggy. Process bread, spring onions, garlic and olive oil in a food processor or blender until combined. Add cucumber and verjuice and blend until combined. Adjust with enough verjuice to form a soup consistency. Adjust the seasoning, then cover with plastic film and chill for a couple of hours or overnight.
- Top each serve with 1 teaspoon of coconut milk and a few mint leaves.

Asparagus with Soft-boiled Eggs and Parmigiano Reggiano

2 bunches thick asparagus, woody ends trimmed and discarded

pinch of caster sugar

sea salt

40 g unsalted butter, melted

4 free-range eggs (as fresh as possible – see page 19 for more information), at room temperature

80–100 g Parmigiano Reggiano, shaved

freshly ground black pepper

SERVES 4

Asparagus are certainly very accessible these days, whether from your own garden, greengrocers or supermarkets – just bear in mind that their natural season is spring. The less asparagus (or any other fruit or vegetable) has to travel, the fresher and tastier it will be. In South Australia asparagus season runs from August until November, or thereabouts. To trim asparagus, simply snap off the woody ends; if you actually hear a crisp 'pop' when doing this, then you can be assured that your asparagus is very fresh (if not, add half a teaspoon of sugar and a little salt to the cooking water – it will help).

One of the things I'd recommend doing is practising your method for soft-boiling eggs. It's such a basic thing, I know, and there are a number of ways people swear by for getting it right, but once you find yours, practise and practise again as a perfect soft-boiled egg can be used in so many ways. Generally, I cook room temperature eggs in a saucepan of simmering water for 2 minutes, then remove from the heat and leave them to stand in the saucepan for another 4 minutes. If your eggs are really fresh they will be difficult to peel.

- Blanch asparagus in a saucepan of salted boiling water for 2–3 minutes or until just tender (add a pinch of caster sugar if you haven't picked the asparagus fresh from your garden). Drain and brush with melted butter.
- Gently place eggs in a saucepan of gently simmering water over low heat and cook for exactly 2 minutes. Remove pan from the heat and leave eggs to stand in the water for 4 minutes precisely. Carefully remove eggs from the pan and leave to cool slightly – this can be sped up by placing the eggs in a bowl of iced water for 5–10 seconds; the iced water will help make them easier to peel, especially if the eggs are very fresh. Carefully peel eggs.
- Divide asparagus among 4 plates, then spoon a little of the melted butter over them. Top each serve with a soft-boiled egg and some shaved Parmigiano Reggiano, then season with salt and pepper and serve.

Maggie's Prawn Cocktail

3 roma tomatoes, halved lengthways

sea salt and freshly ground black pepper

extra virgin olive oil, for cooking

brandy, for drizzling

¼ cup verjuice (or dry white wine or water)

a few sprigs dill, plus extra to serve

a few sprigs lemon verbena (optional)

12 medium or 8 large raw king prawns

½ iceberg lettuce heart, outer leaves discarded and heart cut into strips

⅓ cup mayonnaise (preferably homemade)

lemon wedges, to serve

SERVES 2 AS AN ENTRÉE

Who needs a recipe for a prawn cocktail? Possibly no one, but I've used homemade mayonnaise here instead of the 'cocktail sauce' I grew up with (consisting of whipped cream, tomato sauce and Worcestershire sauce – it is still the one that my daughter Elli asks for). Just add some slow-roasted tomatoes with brandy drizzled over them at the end for their surprise value and suddenly I remember why everything old is new again!

- Preheat fan-forced oven to 150°C (300°F).
- Place tomatoes, cut-side up on a baking tray, then season well with salt and pepper and drizzle with olive oil. Roast for anywhere between 1-4 hours, depending on the level of moisture of the tomatoes. Drizzle with a little brandy and set aside.
- Place verjuice and herbs in a saucepan and bring to a simmer over medium heat. Add prawns and enough water to just cover, then gently poach over low heat until pink and just cooked through. Remove prawns and leave to cool, then peel and clean, leaving 2 unpeeled to garnish each serve, if desired.
- Place lettuce in the base of 2 serving glasses, then add half of the mayonnaise, a few roasted tomatoes and top with half of the prawns. Add remaining mayonnaise, tomatoes and prawns. Drizzle with olive oil mixed with the juices from the roasted tomatoes, then scatter with dill or lemon verbena and serve with a wedge of lemon to the side.

Spring Salad

4 medium-sized new-season waxy potatoes (such as nicolas or kipflers)

extra virgin olive oil, for drizzling

8 tiny zucchini (courgettes)

150 g sugar snap peas

1 kg young broad (fava) bean pods

1½ tablespoons lemon juice

¼ cup walnut oil

sea salt and freshly ground black pepper

200 g mixed salad leaves, washed and dried

150 g goat's curd

½ bunch chives, finely chopped

unsprayed borage flowers (optional), to serve

SERVES 4 AS A LUNCHEON DISH OR ENTRÉE

This salad is about celebrating spring and its lovely produce. Whilst a salad can be served as part of a meal, when it contains as many beautiful ingredients as this one does, I love to serve it on its own as a luncheon dish, or as a prelude to a piece of perfectly grilled fish, chicken or lamb for dinner. When cooking broad beans, after removing the beans from the pods you can either leave them as is or double-peel them, if the vibrant bright green of the peeled beans appeals to you. The flavour differs between the two options, but I must admit that I love them equally both ways.

- Place potatoes in a saucepan, cover with cold water, then bring to the boil and cook for 20 minutes or until tender (the exact time will depend on their age and variety). Drain and cut warm potatoes in half and toss with a little olive oil.
- Bring another saucepan of water to the boil, then blanch zucchini for 2 minutes. Remove zucchini with a slotted spoon, then leave to cool for 3-4 minutes and cut in half lengthways and drizzle with olive oil. Blanch sugar snap peas in the same pan of boiling water for 3 minutes, then drain. Blanch broad bean pods for 3 minutes or until just tender, then drain. Peel broad bean pods, then double-peel beans to remove skins if desired. Drizzle all vegetables with a little olive oil.
- In a large bowl, combine lemon juice, walnut oil and 2 tablespoons olive oil, then season with salt and pepper to taste. Add salad leaves and toss to combine. Place salad leaves on a serving plate. Toss potatoes, zucchini, sugar snap peas, broad beans and goat's curd with a little more olive oil, then season with salt and spoon on top of the leaves. Top with chives and borage flowers, if using, then serve.

Potted Prawns

200 g unsalted butter

1 teaspoon ground mace

1 tablespoon finely chopped French tarragon, plus extra whole leaves, to scatter

500 g cooked medium king prawns (you'll need 250 g picked prawn meat)

1 teaspoon sea salt

½ teaspoon freshly ground black pepper

3 teaspoons verjuice or lemon juice

4 thick slices bread

rocket leaves and lemon wedges, to serve

SERVES 4

'Potting' seafood is such an English thing to do; by this I mean preserving it under a layer of clarified butter to extend its shelf-life. I often wonder why we don't do this more here in Australia, given that so many of us have access to the coast and to fishing, crabbing or prawning as a pastime.

Over the years, I've often found our family seaside holidays to be a time of plenty, so it's good to have a few ideas for 'putting down' some of the catch to see us through at least a couple of days. I'm often surprised by how pristine the potted seafood, in this case prawns, remains under the clarified butter plug; it successfully keeps oxygen, that spoiler of cooked foods, away from the prawns. Here I've used prawns, but this is fabulous made with freshly cooked and picked blue swimmer crab meat too.

- To clarify the butter, heat butter, mace and chopped tarragon in a shallow frying pan over medium heat until butter is nut-brown. Remove from the heat and leave to cool for 15 minutes or until the butter solids separate and the flavours have infused. Carefully pour off and reserve the nut-brown butter, discarding the residue in the pan. Strain butter, discarding tarragon. You should have 160 ml melted clarified butter.

- Peel and clean prawns, removing the veins. Using two forks, shred prawn meat, then mix in salt and pepper. Add verjuice and mix in well. Transfer to a large bowl, then pour in three-quarters of the clarified butter, making sure you leave any solids and water that have separated from the butter behind. Stir through and adjust seasoning, if necessary, then divide prawn mixture between four ½ cup-capacity ramekins or place in a 2-cup capacity mould, pressing down to compact and smoothe the surface with the back of a spoon. Sprinkle over tarragon leaves, then pour enough clarified butter over to seal with a thin layer, making sure that the prawn meat is completely covered. Refrigerate until butter is set, then remove from the refrigerator 10 minutes before serving.

- Just before serving preheat fan-forced oven to 200°C (400°F).

- Brush bread with the remaining clarified butter, then place on a baking tray and bake for 5 minutes or until crisp.

- Serve potted prawns with toast, some rocket leaves and wedges of lemon to the side.

Carrots in Verjuice with Goat's Cheese and Pine Nuts

¼ cup dried currants

⅓ cup verjuice

1 bunch baby (Dutch) carrots, green tops trimmed (leave about 2 cm), scrubbed

sea salt

¼ cup pine nuts

100 g unsalted butter, chopped

¼ cup chopped flat-leaf parsley

½ cup marinated chevre or fresh goat's curd

SERVES 4 AS A LUNCHEON DISH OR AN ACCOMPANIMENT

Over the years I've learnt so much about verjuice, both from my own cooking and that of others – I appreciate the incredible generosity of friends (not to mention complete strangers) who share the numerous ways they've found to cook with this magical ingredient. Here I've used it with carrots – a vegetable I have to admit to not bothering to either grow or seek out, unless I spy a young bunch at our weekly Barossa produce markets. Par-cooking them, then rubbing off their skins and tossing them in nut-brown butter with verjuice gives them a totally different dimension, while still managing to retain their sweetness. Served just like this, this dish is a great accompaniment to any meal, but the addition of currants, pine nuts and goat's cheese transforms it into a wonderful luncheon dish in its own right.

- Place currants and verjuice in a small bowl and leave to plump.
- Cook carrots in a saucepan of boiling salted water until almost cooked through. (The exact time depends on the freshness and size of the carrots, but I find that after about 5 minutes is a good time to check. To do this, remove a carrot from the pan, then rub with a clean Chux; if cooked, the skin will easily peel off.) Leave carrots to cool a little, then use a Chux to rub skins off while still warm. Set peeled carrots aside to cool, then halve lengthways.
- Drain currants, reserving verjuice.
- Toast pine nuts in a frying pan over low heat until light brown. Transfer to a bowl, then add butter to the pan and melt over medium heat until bubbling but not nut-brown. Add carrots to the pan and increase heat to high, then cook for 2–3 minutes or until butter turns nut-brown. Add reserved verjuice and cook until reduced and syrupy. Add currants, pine nuts and parsley, then transfer to a serving dish. Top with chevre or spoon over goat's curd and serve at once.

Olive Tart

350 g bought butter puff pastry,
thawed (I use Carême, made here in
the Barossa)

1 free-range egg, lightly beaten

2 whole heads garlic, cloves separated

extra virgin olive oil, for drizzling

1 cup black olives, pitted

zest of 1 orange, finely peeled with
a potato peeler

1 tablespoon rosemary leaves

2 tablespoons oregano, roughly chopped

80 g marinated Persian goat's feta

oregano leaves, to serve

SERVES 6-8

It's no secret that I love olives and extra virgin olive oil, and that I am always seeking new ways to use them, such as in this tart. But I have to say the real hero of this dish is the fresh local garlic. From November through to about February or March in the Barossa, the young Marschall boys sell their highly sought after heads of fresh pink-hued garlic at our local produce markets. After using such amazing garlic, I am unable to bring myself to use the bleached imported stuff that is so inferior – if the local garlic isn't available I actually stop to think whether I want to add garlic to a dish at all, it is just so good. Seek out local garlic at specialty farmers' markets, if you can, during summer. It keeps for months if stored in a dry, dark, airy spot.

- Roll out pastry until 2.5 mm thick. Cut a 3 cm wide strip from each side of the pastry sheet. Place the trimmed pastry sheet on a baking tray lined with baking paper, then position the 4 strips on the pastry sheet to create a border. Prick the base of the pastry thoroughly with a fork. Refrigerate for several hours, or if you're in a hurry, pop in the freezer for 15 minutes.

- Blanch garlic cloves in a saucepan of boiling water for 5 minutes. Drain, leave until cool enough to handle, then peel; the skins will easily slip off after cooking. Place peeled garlic in the smallest frying pan you have, drizzle generously with olive oil, cover and simmer over low heat for 10-15 minutes or until golden, then leave to cool.

- Preheat fan-forced oven to 220°C (450°F).

- Brush pastry border with beaten egg. Bake pastry for 20 minutes, then remove from oven and dot with peeled garlic. Toss olives with orange zest, oregano, rosemary leaves, if using, and a drizzle of olive oil, then scatter evenly over pastry base. Bake for 10 minutes, then reduce oven temperature to 200°C (400°F) and bake for another 10 minutes or until pastry is deep golden.

- Place spoonfuls of goat's feta over the filling, add a final drizzle of olive oil, then scatter with oregano leaves and serve.

Haloumi and Citrus Lentils

juice of 1 orange (about 100 ml)

2 limes, 1 very thinly sliced and cut into small wedges and 1 juiced

220 g green lentils

sea salt and freshly ground black pepper

extra virgin olive oil, for drizzling

1 cup chopped coriander (optional)

300 g haloumi, cut lengthways into 12 slices

plain flour, for dusting

coriander sprigs, to serve

SERVES 4 AS A LUNCHEON DISH

Until I experienced the delight of eating fresh new-season lentils I used to think lentils had to be disguised to be worth cooking – now I can be a hippie too! Although you may think I am disguising them here by cooking them with citrus juice, I think the acidity is a great counterpoint to their earthiness. Yes, I know that haloumi can be chewy, but it is nicely so if not overcooked (when it is just plain tough). While this dish offers a really good combination of flavours, it would be nothing without a final flourish of excellent extra virgin olive oil before serving.

- Combine orange and lime juice, then place ½ cup combined citrus juice and 1.5 litres water in a medium-sized saucepan and bring to the boil. Add lentils, then return to the boil, reduce heat to low and cook for 20–25 minutes or until al dente. Drain lentils, add 2 tablespoons of the remaining citrus juice and lime wedges, then season with salt and pepper and drizzle generously with olive oil. Leave covered to keep warm.

- Make a dressing by combining remaining citrus juice with ½ cup olive oil, then add chopped coriander, if using, and season to taste with salt and pepper.

- Place a frying pan over high heat until hot. Toss haloumi in flour seasoned with salt and pepper, then fry in a little olive oil for about 40 seconds or until golden, then turn and repeat. Take care not to overcook or it will be too chewy. Remove from the pan and drizzle with a little of the dressing.

- Add remaining dressing to lentils and stir to mix, then divide between 4 plates. Top each plate with pan-fried haloumi. Scatter with coriander sprigs and serve.

Zucchini Flowers

6 large zucchini (courgette) flowers, trimmed, stamens removed

100 g gruth (a soft, fresh cheese made here in the Barossa) or fresh ricotta or Meredith Dairy goat's curd (sold as Cargarie)

1 tablespoon finely chopped chives

3 anchovy fillets, drained and finely chopped

freshly ground black pepper

vegetable oil, for deep-frying

semolina, for dusting

sea salt

1 cup buttermilk

SERVES 2 AS AN ENTRÉE

Zucchini flowers still seem a little exotic to some cooks, but all you need to do to feel that they are easily within your reach is to grow your own zucchinis and see how abundant the flowers are. If harvesting your own I'd recommend checking the flowers carefully for ants as they often seem to congregate closely in the base of the blossoms. The flowers sold in containers still attached to tiny zucchini are blissfully ant-free and, if bought really fresh, are great. Zucchini flowers are very fragile, so cook them as close to picking or buying as you can.

The size of the flowers used determines how much filling you will need. The amount I've given here is for six large flowers. However, when I cooked this recently using a packet of bought zucchini flowers with zucchinis still attached, they were very small, so I only needed half of the filling.

- If the zucchinis attached to the flowers are large, remove them; if they are small (finger size), leave them attached.

- Mix cheese, chives and anchovies together, then season with a little pepper. Gently open each flower, then place 1 heaped teaspoon of the mixture inside each one, taking care not to tear the petals. Pinch gently to close, then twist to seal in the filling.

- Heat enough oil to deep-fry in a medium saucepan over high heat until hot. Season semolina with sea salt and freshly ground black pepper. Dust each flower in seasoned semolina and dip into buttermilk. Repeat this process once again to create a thick batter. Working in batches, deep-fry zucchini flowers for a few minutes or until golden, then drain on paper towels and serve immediately.

Beetroot, Pear and Celery Heart Salad

8 baby beetroot, stalks trimmed

50-70 ml extra virgin olive oil, plus extra for drizzling

sea salt and freshly ground black pepper

¼ cup vino cotto

⅓ cup walnuts

1 tablespoon wholegrain mustard

2 tablespoons red-wine vinegar

1 teaspoon caster sugar

2 large or 4 small ripe pears

juice of 1 lemon

2 celery hearts (pale inner sticks and leaves)

200 g salad burnett or other salad leaves

SERVES 4 AS AN ENTRÉE

I've already declared my feelings about beetroot, and I must like pears as I have so many pear trees in my own orchard, but the success of this dish is really driven by the celery hearts. Good, fresh, crisp celery is hugely under-rated and what's worse is that many people throw the tender pale inner hearts away, which is the part I love best, either raw or cooked. Add some lovely salad leaves and you're in business. Throw in some good local blue cheese or goat's cheese or imported gorgonzola and you've got lunch.

- Preheat fan-forced oven to 180°C (350°F).
- Wash and dry beetroot and place on a baking tray. Drizzle with olive oil, then season with salt and pepper and cover with foil. Bake for 90 minutes or until tender; they are cooked when you can easily insert a skewer. Leave to cool a little, then peel as soon as they are cool enough to handle. Drizzle with vino cotto, then set aside to cool completely.
- Place walnuts on a baking tray and roast for 10 minutes, checking frequently to make sure they don't burn. Immediately wrap in a clean tea towel, then rub to peel off skins. Sift rubbed walnuts through a sieve to get rid of skins, then leave to cool. Roughly chop cooled walnuts and set aside.
- Spoon mustard into a small bowl, add vinegar and mix well, then slowly add the olive oil, stirring continuously to emulsify (or you can place the ingredients in a jar, seal with a lid and shake). Stir in salt, pepper and sugar, then adjust seasoning, if required.
- Slice pears in half, then cut into eighths, removing the core as you go, then squeeze with lemon juice to prevent browning. Thinly slice celery hearts on the diagonal, incorporating as many of the leaves as possible. Mix sliced pears and celery hearts with 2-3 tablespoons dressing.
- Cut beetroot in half and divide among 4 plates, then top with pear and celery mixture, salad burnett or other leaves and walnuts and season to taste. Serve immediately.

Broad Beans with Pecorino

2 kg young broad (fava) bean pods, podded

sea salt

⅓ cup extra virgin olive oil, plus extra for drizzling

4 thick slices sourdough

2 tablespoons roughly chopped mint

freshly ground black pepper

80-100 g pecorino, shaved

SERVES 4 AS AN ENTRÉE

This has to be one of the simplest dishes ever. It requires fresh young broad beans, which means making it in August or thereabouts, as this is the time they start appearing on greengrocers' shelves. You can pod them, then eat them either raw, like this (in which case, they must be very young), or purée them with a good splash of extra virgin olive oil and some grated pecorino – the latter would form a chunky paste, ideal for spreading on a good piece of bruschetta.

- Blanch broad beans in a saucepan of boiling salted water for 3 minutes. Drain and leave until cool enough to handle, then double-peel and drizzle with olive oil.
- Heat a char-grill pan until hot, then brush sourdough with olive oil and grill on each side until well toasted.
- Toss broad beans with mint and olive oil and season to taste with salt and pepper. Spoon broad bean mixture onto grilled sourdough, then top with shaved pecorino and another drizzle of olive oil.
- Serve immediately.

Braised Waxy Potatoes

500 g waxy potatoes (such as nicolas, dutch creams or kipflers), halved or quartered, depending on their size

1½ cups chicken stock

2 fresh bay leaves

40 g unsalted butter, chopped

extra virgin olive oil, for cooking

sea salt

1 tablespoon finely chopped thyme

¼ cup roughly chopped flat-leaf parsley

squeeze of lemon juice

freshly ground black pepper

SERVES 2-3 AS AN ACCOMPANIMENT

Although this isn't the most beautiful dish to look at, I wanted to show you how it turns out (see opposite). It's one of those surprise dishes because it is so incredibly tasty – with not even a dash of cream added. The secret to its success is the flavour of the potatoes you use. For me, nicolas are the first variety I seek out, perhaps because they are grown here in the Barossa. From late January, when nicolas are in season, I'm first in the queue at the potato stall at our local Saturday markets. When cooked and cut into, their flesh is a deep yellowy gold and tastes just like the potatoes I grew to love during my time in Italy.

This is such a delicious dish that it deserves to be served as the star of a meal in its own right. It only needs something really simple alongside – a perfectly grilled lamb chop for instance, or the Beef in the Italian Style on page 124.

- Preheat fan-forced oven to 180°C (350°F).
- Place potatoes in a small deep baking dish so that they fit snugly; they need to be submerged by the stock. Add stock, bay leaves, butter and a good splash of olive oil, along with a pinch or two of salt. Bake, uncovered, for 60–90 minutes or until tender (the exact time will depend on the variety and size of potatoes used), basting with cooking liquid every now and again.
- Sprinkle with thyme, parsley and lemon juice, then season to taste and serve.

Smoked Ocean Trout with Potato Pikelets

crème fraîche, for topping

300 g cold-smoked ocean trout (I use Woodbridge Smokehouse Cold-smoked Ocean Trout)

chervil sprigs, to serve

POTATO PIKELETS

300 g waxy potatoes (such as nicolas, dutch creams or kipflers), roughly chopped

100 g plain flour

¼ teaspoon bicarbonate of soda

½ teaspoon cream of tartar

1 free-range egg

150 ml milk

¼ teaspoon finely chopped lemon zest

1 teaspoon finely chopped garlic chives

extra virgin olive oil, for cooking

unsalted butter, for cooking

MAKES 12-15

Whilst there are many brands of smoked salmon and ocean trout on the market, there is nothing quite like the cold-smoked ocean trout made by Woodbridge Smokehouse in Tasmania. Ocean trout has a tighter texture than salmon that I prefer. The flavour of the brined and apple-smoked ocean trout is both delicate and meaty – although perhaps this is because I buy it as a whole piece and carve it myself, and my slices tend to be thicker than the pre-sliced products.

I first heard of Woodbridge Smokehouse when they won the award for 'Best New Product' in the *Vogue Entertaining + Travel*/Audi 2007 Fine Food Awards, of which I am proudly the patron. As a result, I visited them to experience first-hand how they do what they do.

- Bring potatoes to the boil in a saucepan of water, then cook for 15–20 minutes or until tender (the exact time will depend on the age, variety and size). Drain potatoes, then immediately purée with a potato ricer or mouli (a potato masher can be used but the potatoes may be a bit lumpy). Cover with plastic film and leave to cool.
- Sift flour, bicarbonate of soda and cream of tartar into a bowl and make a well in the centre. Add egg, then, using your hands, gently move the flour into the centre of the well, mixing to combine. Slowly add milk, a little at a time, stirring well after each addition until well combined. Gently fold potato purée into the batter, then stir in lemon zest and chives.
- Heat a little olive oil and a knob of butter in a large non-stick frying pan over medium heat. Working in batches, drop a few tablespoonfuls of the mixture into the pan at a time and cook until the bases are golden. Turn over and cook until the other sides are golden. Remove and leave to cool.
- Top pikelets with dollops of crème fraîche and thick pieces of the best cold-smoked ocean trout you can find. Scatter with chervil and serve.

Warm Smoked Chook Salad with Mustard Apricots and Nicola Potatoes

3 nicola or other waxy potatoes (about 300 g)

8 dried apricots

¼ cup verjuice

1 tablespoon mustard powder (I use Keen's)

½ smoked chook

40-60 g unsalted butter

extra virgin olive oil, for cooking

sea salt

1½ cups rocket

1½ cups flat-leaf parsley leaves

freshly ground black pepper

VINAIGRETTE

¼ cup extra virgin olive oil

2 tablespoons vino cotto

1 tablespoon mustard powder (I use Keen's)

SERVES 4 AS A LUNCHEON DISH

I find myself saying this often about ingredients, but will say it again anyway – unless you have top-quality produce there's no point in bothering with this recipe. A good plump smoked chook is what you need here. Larger, fattier chooks are the best ones for smoking as the layer of fat saves them from drying out during the hot-smoking process, resulting in a moist, delicious bird.

The chook I used here was about 1.85 kilograms in all, which means that you'll have a lot of leftover chook meat. You can either double (or even treble) this recipe to serve more, or carve the meat as needed (it keeps longer and stays juicier this way) to make wonderful sandwiches with rye bread and a delicious chutney, such as one made from green tomatoes.

- Cook potatoes in a saucepan of simmering water until tender, then drain and leave to cool. Cut cooled potatoes into 3 slices lengthways.
- Meanwhile, soak apricots in verjuice to reconstitute until nicely plumped, then drain, reserving verjuice. Make a paste by combining the reserved verjuice and mustard powder. Place apricots in this mustard syrup and leave to macerate.
- Carve chook meat off half of a breast, leg and thigh (I think it's important to use a mixture of breast and leg meat for this salad). Cover with plastic film to keep moist and set aside.
- For the vinaigrette, combine the ingredients and set aside.
- Heat butter in a frying pan over medium heat until nut-brown, then add a splash of olive oil to stop it from burning and season with salt. Pan-fry potato slices until crisp and golden, then transfer to paper towels to drain.
- Add another splash of olive oil to the pan, then toss the drained apricots in the pan until caramelised. Remove and set aside. Add a little more olive oil to the pan, then add the smoked chook and toss for 1½-2 minutes or until just warmed through. Return potatoes and apricots to the pan and toss to mix together.
- Transfer chicken mixture to a large bowl, then add rocket and parsley, drizzle with vinaigrette, season with pepper, if desired, and serve.

Saffron Tomato Relish

¾ cup caster sugar

700 ml verjuice

pinch of saffron threads

600 g roma tomatoes

extra virgin olive oil, for cooking

1 onion, roughly chopped

2 cloves garlic, sliced

MAKES ABOUT 2 CUPS

After tasting a saffron-infused tomato relish on a trip to Dubai, I returned home determined to recreate its wonderful flavour. The task was more difficult than I'd imagined, as the saffron intensifies when the relish is stored, overpowering the other flavours. I finally got the balance right and I'm glad that I did – it's a great addition to couscous, served atop grilled fish or poached poultry, or spread on savoury biscuits with cream cheese. I particularly like serving it as quite a different accompaniment to a sharp cheddar or goat's cheese.

♦ Place sugar and verjuice in a stainless steel saucepan and stir over low heat until sugar has dissolved, then bring to the boil over high heat and simmer for 10–12 minutes or until reduced and syrupy. Remove from the heat, then add saffron threads and leave to infuse for 5 minutes.

♦ Cut a shallow cross on the top of each tomato with a small, sharp knife, then briefly blanch tomatoes in a saucepan of boiling water. Transfer to a bowl of iced water immediately to loosen the skins. Leave until cool enough to handle, then slip skins off, cut in half and remove seeds. Set aside.

♦ Heat a little olive oil in a saucepan over medium heat, then add onion and garlic and cook for 10 minutes or until softened. Add tomatoes, verjuice saffron and syrup and cook over low heat for 1½–2 hours, stirring occasionally, until the syrup has reduced and thickened.

♦ Immediately transfer to a sterilised 500 ml jar (see page 27) and seal, then turn upside-down to ensure lid is sterilised by the hot mixture.

♦ Saffron tomato relish will keep in the refrigerator for a few months once opened or unopened in a cool place for up to a year.

Frozen Pea Soup

30 g unsalted butter

extra virgin olive oil, for cooking

4 golden shallots, finely chopped

1 cup chicken stock, plus extra to adjust consistency, if needed

1 × 500 g packet frozen peas

1 stalk chervil, plus extra to serve

½ cup pouring cream

sea salt and freshly ground black pepper

SERVES 4 AS AN ENTRÉE OR 2 AS A MAIN MEAL

Yes, I keep a packet of frozen peas in my freezer! You never know when you are going to be stuck for something to cook. Truth be told, unless you're picking your own peas straight from the garden, fresh peas from the greengrocer will be such a disappointment after all of that podding as the whole flavour changes so much if they're stored after picking. On the other hand, freshly picked and podded peas straight from the garden are one of life's great pleasures – more so because they are so rare.

♦ Melt butter in a deep frying pan with a little olive oil added over medium heat. Add shallots and sauté for 10 minutes or until soft.

♦ Meanwhile, bring chicken stock to the boil in a small saucepan.

♦ Add peas and chervil to frying pan, then stir to combine and cook gently over low heat for 5 minutes or until peas have thawed. Pour hot chicken stock over peas, then bring to the boil over high heat. Remove from the heat and leave to cool slightly.

♦ Process pea mixture in a blender until puréed, add cream and a little extra stock, to adjust the consistency if necessary. Season to taste with salt and pepper, then refrigerate until cold.

♦ Serve bowls of chilled soup topped with a sprig of chervil.

Eggplant Pickle

2 ripe medium-sized eggplants
(aubergines), peeled and thickly sliced

sea salt

¼ cup extra virgin olive oil

2 cloves garlic, chopped

½ cup verjuice

2 tablespoons thinly sliced mint

MAKES 1½–2 CUPS

This recipe is based on a side dish I used to cook at the Pheasant Farm restaurant to serve alongside a simple grilled veal chop or rabbit scaloppine. The trick is to use as little of the oil as you need, then, after you've added the verjuice and reduced it, to wait until you've removed the pan from the heat before adding the mint. Although this pickle is best served on the day it is made, it will last a few days in the refrigerator.

The size and weight of eggplants do not necessarily correspond – older, more deeply coloured, shinier eggplant can weigh half as much as a younger eggplant of roughly the same size. As a result, I like to give the dimensions of the eggplant I use, rather than a weight. In this case, the eggplants were about 12 cm long by 8 cm at their widest point.

• Place eggplant slices in a colander, then sprinkle with salt and leave to drain for 20 minutes; this helps prevent them from absorbing excessive oil during cooking (for more information on whether or not to salt eggplant, see page 19). Wash off salt and thoroughly pat dry with paper towels. Cut eggplant slices into thin strips.

• Heat a little of the oil in a large frying pan over high heat until hot, then, working in batches, fry eggplant strips, adding oil as needed to stop them from sticking to the base of the pan and transferring cooked eggplant to paper towels to drain off excess oil. Return eggplant slices to pan, add garlic and place over high heat. Add verjuice, stir to combine, then bring to the boil and cook until verjuice has evaporated, taking care not to burn garlic.

• Transfer eggplant to a shallow bowl, then add mint and leave to marinate. Serve at room temperature.

Eggplant, Roasted Tomato and 'Rag' Pasta with Buffalo Mozzarella

extra virgin olive oil, for drizzling

¼ cup roughly chopped oregano

8 roma tomatoes, halved lengthways

sea salt and freshly ground black pepper

2 eggplants (aubergines), about 12 × 8 cm, peeled and cut widthways into 2 cm wide slices

sea salt

1 clove garlic, finely chopped

¼ cup basil leaves, plus extra to serve

200 g buffalo mozzarella or chevre, at room temperature and torn

FRESH PASTA

500 g strong plain flour

1 teaspoon sea salt

4 × 61 g free-range eggs

1-2 free-range egg yolks

SERVES 4 AS AN ENTRÉE

With the hot dry conditions we've experienced over the past few Barossan summers eggplant has become the absolute star of my garden. This year I've grown four different varieties, so I've found lots of ways to feature it in my cooking.

Fortuitously, between late summer and autumn is also the perfect time of year to marry eggplant with slow-roasted tomatoes. Then there's the addition of buffalo mozzarella. Although I didn't need any convincing about using it, a recent visit to Victoria's Shaw River Buffalo Cheese, where I actually experienced the sheer delight of being part of the mozzarella making, has made me a lifelong advocate of this cheese. Homemade rag pasta has to be one of the best things to prepare with a helper in tow and it transforms the simple flavours of this dish into something quite spectacular.

- Preheat fan-forced oven to 150°C (300°F).

- Place tomatoes, cut-sides up, on a baking tray, then scatter with 1 tablespoon of the oregano, drizzle with olive oil and season with salt and pepper. Roast for anywhere between 1-4 hours, depending on the level of moisture of the tomatoes.

- For the fresh pasta, mix flour with salt, then spread it on a bench over an area 30 cm in diameter. Make a well in the centre, leaving a bank of flour around the edge. Break eggs into the well, then add yolks, as needed. Using one hand, combine the eggs and yolks until they're amalgamated, and then, using a fork held in the other hand, scoop the flour a little at a time from the flour 'banks' into the egg mixture, incorporating eggs and flour with your hand. If you feel the mixture is too dry, add the remaining egg yolk, working it in the same way. Keep doing this until the mixture becomes a paste.

- Scrape up flour and dough, 'cutting' it until the mixture is well combined. This involves gathering the mass and smearing it across the bench with a pastry scraper until it comes together. Knead the dough for 6-10 minutes, pushing it away from you with the heel of your hand, then turning it a quarter to the right, folding the dough over, pushing it away and so on.

- Once the dough is shiny and silky, roll it into a ball and wrap it in plastic film. Rest dough in the refrigerator for 30 minutes.

- Place a pasta machine on a bench, screwing it down firmly. Cut dough into 10 even pieces and cover with a tea towel. Take one piece of dough and press it as flat as you can with the palm of your hand or a rolling pin, then feed it through the rollers set on their widest aperture. Fold dough in thirds, then pass the narrow end through the machine again. Repeat several times, preferably until you hear a sound that I can only describe as a 'plop' – this is the tension of the dough releasing as it goes through the rollers.

- Adjust the machine to the next setting and pass the dough through. Repeat this with every setting until you get to the last, and finest, one. As the dough moves through each setting the sheets will become finer and finer; you may need to cut the sheets into smaller pieces to make them more manageable. Repeat this process with the remaining dough.

- Cut pasta sheets into irregular pieces or 'rags', then cover with a tea towel and set aside.

- Meanwhile, if desired, soak sliced eggplant in salted water (I usually add 1 tablespoon salt to every 600 ml water) for 30 minutes; this helps prevent it from absorbing excessive oil during cooking (for more information on whether or not to salt eggplant, see page 19).

- Working in batches, fry eggplant in a splash of olive oil in a hot frying pan until cooked, then drain on paper towels. Place warm eggplant, garlic, remaining oregano and basil in a bowl and toss.
- Bring a large saucepan of water to the boil and add a generous amount of salt. Cook the 'rags' for about 3 minutes, then drain and tip back into the pan (you may also want to reserve a little of the cooking water to bind the sauce) and drizzle with olive oil.
- Place pasta, eggplant mixture, roasted tomatoes and half of the mozzarella in a large bowl, season to taste and gently combine.
- Divide pasta between 4 plates, top with the remaining mozzarella, then serve with a final drizzle of olive oil and perhaps a few extra basil leaves.

Baked Savoury Cheesecake

250 g savoury biscuits
(I use 125 g each water crackers
and Arnott's Breton crackers)

125 g unsalted butter, chopped

olive oil spray, for greasing

FILLING

4 free-range eggs

2 tablespoons chopped rosemary

2 tablespoons chopped flat-leaf parsley

finely grated zest of 2 large oranges
(about 2 tablespoons)

8 large green olives, pitted and chopped

250 g fresh ricotta

250 g sour cream

2 teaspoons lemon juice

½ teaspoon sea salt

½ teaspoon freshly ground black pepper

SERVES 6-8 AS A LUNCHEON DISH

Savoury tarts suit my palate. The orange zest is what makes this one sing, and the saltiness of the olives is a great match. Originally I thought I'd call this a quiche, but somehow it didn't seem right – maybe it's because of the addition of ricotta. It makes a good luncheon dish, but I urge you to try serving it well chilled and cut into thin wedges to accompany an aperitif.

- Preheat fan-forced oven to 160°C (325°F).
- Pulse biscuits in a food processor until they resemble fine breadcrumbs. Melt butter and mix thoroughly into crumbled biscuits. Spray a 20 cm springform cake pan with olive oil spray, then press in biscuit mixture firmly to create a crust. Bake for 10 minutes.
- Meanwhile, for the filling, mix eggs, herbs, orange zest and olives. Place ricotta, sour cream and lemon juice in a bowl and stir to combine. Add ricotta mixture to egg mixture, then season with salt and pepper and gently fold with a large metal spoon or a spatula to combine, taking care not to over-mix. Pour mixture into biscuit crust and bake for 40-50 minutes or until the mixture sets. The exact time depends on the dimensions of your pan; for example a 22 cm pan will take about 40 minutes, whereas a 20 cm pan with higher sides may need a bit longer.
- Leave cheesecake to settle in the pan for 10-20 minutes (this makes it easier to cut), then serve either right away or chilled.

Oat, Buttermilk and Honey Pancakes

1½ cups buttermilk

1½ cups rolled oats (I use Four Leaf Milling Organic Rolled Oats from Tarlee)

2 tablespoons honey

1 free-range egg

1 free-range egg yolk

¼ cup extra virgin olive oil

½ cup self-raising flour

1 × 2 cm stick cinnamon, finely ground or ground cinnamon, to taste

sea salt

unsalted butter, for cooking

SERVES 4 FOR BRUNCH

Although this is more of a brunch dish than an entrée, I wanted to include these pancakes anyway as they offer real flavour and texture. I find it a great recipe to make with my grandchildren. Some children (and adults, too) resist trying anything new, but I've found that involving them in the cooking can make all the difference – and, just as importantly, it's fun! I like to serve these with grilled bananas or peaches, depending on the season.

The batter is best made the night before and refrigerated.

- Pour buttermilk over oats and leave for 10 minutes. Add honey, egg, egg yolk and olive oil and stir.
- Sift self-raising flour into another bowl, then add ground cinnamon and a pinch of salt. Add oat mixture to flour mixture and combine well. Leave for at least 1 hour in the refrigerator before cooking, but overnight is best.
- Place a small piece of butter in a frying pan over medium heat and melt until it sizzles. Pour a ladleful of mixture into the pan and cook until golden brown underneath, then flip over and cook until golden. Repeat with remaining mixture, adding more butter to the pan if necessary.
- Leave to cool a little, then serve.

Warm Salad of Guinea Fowl with Orange, Livers and Walnuts

1 × 900 g guinea fowl, legs almost cut away from the frame but still attached (ask your butcher to do this if you like)

½ cup walnuts

sea salt

20 g unsalted butter

extra virgin olive oil, for cooking

¼ cup verjuice

1 orange

3 heads witlof, outer leaves discarded and inner leaves washed and dried

1 small head radicchio, outer leaves discarded and inner leaves picked, washed and dried

MARINADE

1 heaped tablespoon juniper berries, crushed

1 clove garlic, sliced

4 fresh bay leaves, crushed

2 teaspoons thyme leaves

⅓ cup extra virgin olive oil

zest of 1 orange, removed in wide strips with a potato peeler

2 tablespoons orange juice

sea salt

LIVER 'STUFFING'

2½ rashers sugar-cured bacon, rind removed and roughly chopped

unsalted butter, for cooking

extra virgin olive oil, for cooking

180 g chicken livers, connective tissue trimmed, and kept in large pieces

sea salt and freshly ground black pepper

1½ tablespoons finely chopped thyme

⅓ cup prunes, pitted

1 teaspoon roughly chopped rosemary

juice of 1 orange

DRESSING

2 tablespoons extra virgin olive oil

¼ cup walnut oil

1 tablespoon vino cotto

squeeze of lemon juice

sea salt and freshly ground black pepper

SERVES 4 AS A LIGHT MEAL

I wish that we could breed guinea fowl in Australia as well as they manage to in Europe. It comes down to a question of genetics, and the lack of new stock to the guinea fowl gene pool here is not likely to change given the high cost of importing eggs through the quarantine process. However, if you manage to find a local farmer who feeds their guinea fowl a corn diet, you'll get the best bird available – one that is really worth taking the trouble to cook. Guinea fowl breast meat is less plump than that of pheasant, but it is sweeter. Certainly the French would eat guinea fowl before pheasant any day, unlike me, who loves both birds when they are well-bred. Although they have their differences, most recipes for both can be used interchangeably.

- Place guinea fowl in a bowl with marinade ingredients and leave to marinate for 2 hours, turning occasionally.
- Preheat fan-forced oven to 180°C (350°F).
- Place walnuts on a baking tray and roast for 10 minutes, checking frequently to make sure they don't burn. Immediately wrap in a clean tea towel, then rub to peel off skins. Sift rubbed walnuts through a sieve to get rid of skins, then leave to cool. Roughly chop cooled walnuts and set aside.
- Pat guinea fowl skin dry with paper towels, then season generously with salt. Heat butter and a splash of olive oil in a frying pan over medium heat, then add guinea fowl and gently brown all over. Place guinea fowl on its back in a roasting pan and roast for 10 minutes, then turn over onto one side and roast for another 10 minutes. Finally turn onto its other side and roast for another 10 minutes. To test whether it is cooked, insert a skewer into the thickest part of the thigh joint; the juices should run clear. If juices are still pink, continue cooking until juices are clear. Turn guinea fowl upside down, then tip verjuice over and leave to rest, uncovered, in a warm place until cool enough to carve off the bone. Reserve any pan juices.
- For the 'stuffing', fry bacon in a frying pan over high heat for 2-3 minutes or until crisp, then drain on paper towels to remove excess oil. Add a knob of butter and splash of olive oil to the pan, then, when the butter foams, add livers and toss quickly; take care as livers tend to spit when added to a hot pan. Season with salt and pepper, then add thyme and cook for 50 seconds or so; you still want livers to be pink in the middle. Remove from the pan, and leave to rest in a warm place. Wipe pan clean with paper towels, then heat a little more butter and add prunes and rosemary and stir to combine. Deglaze pan with orange juice, then remove from heat and set aside.
- For the dressing, combine all the ingredients plus ¼ cup reserved guinea fowl pan juices.
- To segment the orange, cut a slice from the top and bottom, then cut away the peel, including the bitter white pith. Using a small, sharp knife, cut down one side of an orange segment, then down the other side, releasing it from the membrane. Repeat with remaining segments and set aside, discarding the membrane.
- Carve guinea fowl, then place in a bowl with the liver 'stuffing', walnuts, orange segments, witlof, radicchio and enough of the dressing to coat and gently combine. Transfer to a serving platter or divide among 4 plates and serve immediately.

Verjuice and Avocado Jellies

1½ cups verjuice

1 tablespoon caster sugar

½ bunch chervil, plus extra leaves to serve

2½ × 2 g gelatine leaves

1½ large avocados (such as Reids), peeled and cut into 2 cm pieces (to yield about 300 g avocado pieces)

verjuice or lemon juice, for drizzling

sea salt

extra virgin olive oil and mâche (lamb's lettuce) or rocket leaves (optional), to serve

SERVES 6

I've decided that this dish (or variations thereof) stands as one of my core recipes. Ever since I made my first verjuice jelly, I've made so many variations on the theme, using what seems like every vegetable imaginable and loads of different types of seafood. In the height of summer, when tomatoes are at their seasonal best, some of the avocado component can be replaced with chopped vine-ripened tomatoes. It's a very easy dish to make, especially once you have the confidence to work with gelatine leaves; even I have to admit that they scared me for a long time. It was only after watching someone squeeze the soaked leaves that I realised it was child's play.

Whilst this is great made as one large jelly in a communal dish to share, my favourite way of making it is to prepare individual jellies, which means using a little less gelatine than I'd use if making one large mould (two and a half of the 2 gram leaves for individual moulds or three of the 2 gram leaves for one large mould). It is worth noting that if you are making this on a hot summer's day the amount of gelatine may need to be increased to three leaves so the jelly doesn't melt too quickly if eating it outside.

I urge you to make these jellies as the perfect start to any meal between spring and autumn - but then again, why not winter as well!

- Bring verjuice and sugar to the boil, then remove from heat immediately. Transfer to a bowl, add chervil and leave to infuse.

- Soak gelatine leaves in a bowl of cold water for 5 minutes or until softened, then squeeze out the excess moisture. Strain warm verjuice mixture, then add softened gelatine and stir until gelatine melts. Leave verjuice and gelatine mixture to cool completely.

- Drizzle avocado with verjuice or lemon juice to prevent browning.

- Place a few chervil leaves in the bases of six 100 ml ramekins (or a 600 ml dish - I use a glass jelly bowl). Top with chopped avocado, then pour one-sixth of cooled verjuice mixture over each (or all if using a large bowl). Cover closely with plastic film, then refrigerate for at least 2 hours if using ramekins or 4 hours if using one large bowl, or until set.

- To turn jellies out, stand ramekins in a bowl or baking dish of hot water for 25 seconds to loosen, then invert onto small plates (or one large one for a large jelly).

- Sprinkle jellies with sea salt, then drizzle with olive oil and serve garrnished with a little mâche or rocket leaves, if desired.

Grilled Octopus in Herb Paste with Rouille

800 g giant octopus tentacles
(about 3 tentacles from a large octopus)

extra virgin olive oil, for cooking

lemon wedges, sea salt and freshly
ground black pepper, to serve

MARINADE

¼ cup extra virgin olive oil

2 cloves garlic, roughly chopped

1½ cups flat-leaf parsley, roughly chopped

1 tablespoon chopped marjoram

1 tablespoon salted capers, rinsed

finely grated zest and juice of ½ lemon

ROUILLE

1 ripe large red capsicum (pepper)

2 slices white bread, crusts removed

milk, for soaking

3 threads saffron

¼ teaspoon smoked paprika

3 cloves garlic, chopped

50 ml lemon juice

1 teaspoon Dijon mustard

2 free-range egg yolks

sea salt and freshly ground black pepper

200 ml extra virgin olive oil

1 tablespoon boiling water (optional)

SERVES 6

Cooking an entire octopus is something I actually love to do but I realise that the task is a mite more approachable when you cook just a few tentacles at a time. Whilst I encourage you to make sure your fishmonger has 'tumbled' the octopus well (usually in a cement mixer used specifically for this purpose), I always have a back-up plan as, if not tenderised, octopus will remain tough and be a total disappointment. I'd always known that kiwifruit and paw paw in particular have the ability to 'break down' the structure of meat, tenderising it in the process, so why not octopus too?

Many years ago, I had an opportunity to test out this theory when Stephanie and I prepared a whole menu for a week in Serge Dansereau's restaurant kitchen at what was then Sydney's Regent Hotel, as part of the launch for *Stephanie Alexander and Maggie Beer's Tuscan Cookbook*. Octopus was on the menu but the octopus that arrived from South Australia just didn't 'feel' right to me. I called for kiwifruit, which luckily is readily available, and within thirty minutes of it being sliced and added to the octopus it had achieved the desired effect of tenderising the flesh so the octopus was all that I'd hoped for. It's a handy little trick worth keeping up your sleeve.

- Preheat fan-forced oven to 200°C (400°F).
- For the rouille, place capsicum on a baking tray and roast for 5-10 minutes or until the skin blackens and the capsicum collapses. Remove from oven, then leave to cool for a few minutes before placing it in a plastic bag to sweat. When capsicum is cool enough to handle, peel and discard skin, then remove seeds. Meanwhile, soak bread in a little milk with the saffron threads for 10 minutes, then squeeze thoroughly to remove excess moisture. Process capsicum, bread, paprika, garlic, lemon juice, mustard and egg yolks in a food processor until puréed, then season to taste with salt and pepper. With the motor running, pour in olive oil in a thin, steady stream until the mixture thickens and emulsifies. Only add boiling water to thin if you feel it is necessary. Set aside.
- Process marinade ingredients in a food processor until a smooth paste forms, then set aside.
- Remove and discard blackened skin from octopus tentacles by pulling it away, leaving tentacles intact. Smother tentacles in marinade paste, coating them thoroughly.
- Heat a char-grill pan over high heat until smoking and brush with olive oil, then cook the octopus on each side for 2 minutes or until char-grill marks appear; resist the temptation to turn it before this. Turn and repeat on the other side. Remove from the heat and drizzle with a little olive oil. Season octopus with salt and pepper to taste, then add a squeeze of lemon juice and leave to rest for a few minutes.
- Cut octopus into bite-sized pieces, then drizzle with olive oil and serve with a spoonful of rouille to the side.

Middle

Grilled Squid au Naturel

4 small frozen squid, almost thawed

extra virgin olive oil, for drizzling

1 lemon, sliced widthways

1 teaspoon dried Greek oregano (rigani) (optional)

2 tablespoons salted capers, rinsed and drained

squeeze of lemon juice and roughly chopped flat-leaf parsley, to serve

SERVES 4

It is comforting to know that squid is one ingredient that is all the better for having been frozen, as it is tenderised in the process. Another benefit of freezing becomes apparent when it comes time to clean them. As this is not everyone's favourite task (indeed, it actually seems to bring some people out in a rash), it is made all the easier by partially thawing the squid first – this way you can pull out all the intestines in one go and not even bother to clean the outsides. The saltiness of the skins means that the squid don't need to be seasoned with salt before cooking.

- To prepare squid, gently pull the whole of their guts out in one piece, along with the cartilage bone; this task is much easier when the squid have not thawed completely. Leave their skins on. Use a teaspoon with a long handle to check that the squid tubes are completely clean.
- Heat a char-grill pan or barbecue grill-plate as hot as possible.
- Drizzle squid with olive oil, then scatter with oregano, if using, and place on the hot char-grill pan or barbecue grill-plate. Cook each side of the squid for about 90 seconds, turning several times to make sure each side makes contact with the grill plate and begins to caramelise (a total of 4–5 minutes for small squid). The skin will be a lovely crazed burgundy colour.
- Take the squid off the grill-plate and leave to rest for the same amount of time as you cooked them.
- Brush lemon slices with olive oil, then cook on the hot grill-plate until caramelised.
- Drizzle generously with more olive oil, then scatter with capers, squeeze with lemon juice and serve scattered with chopped flat-leaf parsley, with grilled lemon to the side.

Southern Herrings in Vine Leaves

½ cup roughly chopped marjoram

½ cup roughly chopped flat-leaf parsley

2 tablespoons salted capers, rinsed

1 tablespoon rinsed and finely chopped preserved lemon rind

extra virgin olive oil, for cooking

8-12 grape vine leaves (I use blanched fresh ones but preserved vine leaves could be used instead)

4 × 400 g southern herrings, cleaned and scaled

sea salt

4 handfuls wild fennel or 2 handfuls dill sprigs

lemon wedges, to serve

SERVES 4

I've used southern herrings (formerly known as tommy ruffs) to show how the principle of cooking in vine leaves can be applied to any small fish. I must say that the results when using a kettle barbecue are tremendous, as the heat isn't as fierce as that of a gas barbecue. Instead of barbecuing, the fish can also be cooked in an oiled baking dish on a bed of wild fennel or dill in a 230°C (475°F) oven for 10 minutes, then turned and cooked for another 5 minutes.

Sometimes I use blanched leek strips to tie the parcels, but kitchen string can be used instead.

- Pound marjoram, parsley, capers, preserved lemon rind and enough olive oil to form a paste with a mortar and pestle or blend in a food processor.
- Place 2-3 overlapping large vine leaves on a chopping board and spread with one-quarter of the paste; the layer of vine leaves should be large enough to wrap completely around a fish. Repeat with remaining vine leaves and paste.
- Place a fish on each set of vine leaves, then wrap securely, tying the parcels with kitchen string. Drizzle with olive oil and sprinkle with salt.
- Heat a barbecue or char-grill plate until very hot, then cook the fish parcels for 12-14 minutes, turning 3 times during cooking, or until the fish are cooked through at their thickest parts.
- Leave to rest for 5 minutes, then serve on a bed of wild fennel or dill, with lemon wedges to the side.

Asparagus and Leek Tart

olive oil spray, for greasing

unsalted butter, for cooking

2 fat leeks, white parts only, thinly sliced

sea salt and freshly ground black pepper

8 fat spears asparagus
(or 12 thinner ones), bases trimmed

2 tablespoons coarsely chopped
flat-leaf parsley

14 free-range egg yolks

2½ cups pouring cream

60 g grated Parmigiano Reggiano

SOUR-CREAM PASTRY

250 g plain flour

200 g chilled unsalted butter, chopped

120 ml sour cream

SERVES 8

I decided to cook this tart after a recent visit to Paris. Just around the corner from our delightful but tiny hotel in the sixth arrondisement, near the Church of St Sulpice, is Mulot's Patisserie (I still dream of their coffee-cream macaroons and, as you know, I don't even have a sweet tooth). We decided to have a picnic in our room with the balcony doors open to the wonderful view, so Mulot's was naturally our first stop in procuring supplies. I bought an asparagus-dotted tart the custard of which was simply luscious, and certainly more extravagant than any quiche I'd ever eaten.

This recipe is my attempt to create something similar, hence the use of fourteen egg yolks. My guilt at having all those egg whites left over was somewhat assuaged as I was making pavlova for a party at the same time. Of course, if you are not in a pavlova-making frenzy, egg whites freeze brilliantly – just remember to clearly label the container with the number, weight and date and use them within three months.

This doesn't require all of the pastry, so with the remnants I roll the other piece out, blind bake it (see page 16), then top it with caramelised onions, anchovies and flat-leaf parsley for a light lunch or supper.

- For the sour-cream pastry, process flour and butter in a food processor until it resembles coarse breadcrumbs. With the motor running, gradually add about two-thirds of the sour cream at first, then only add enough of the remaining sour cream to help the pastry just come together to form a ball. Turn out onto a lightly floured bench and bring it together into a rectangle with your hands. Divide the pastry in two, with one piece slightly larger than the other. Wrap both pieces in plastic film. Chill the larger piece in the refrigerator for at least 20 minutes and freeze the other piece for later use.

- Spray a 24 cm springform cake pan with olive oil spray. Roll out pastry until 3 mm thick and use to line the pan, bringing pastry up past the rim to allow for some shrinkage when it cooks. Prick pastry base with a fork, then line with foil and fill with pastry weights and chill in the refrigerator for at least 1 hour.

- Preheat fan-forced oven to 220°C (450°F).

- Bake pastry shell for 12 minutes or until just lightly coloured. Remove the foil and weights and bake for another 5 minutes or until the pastry is cooked through and looks dry. Remove from oven and set aside.

- Reduce oven temperature to 160°C (325°F).

- While the pastry is baking, heat a large knob of butter in a frying pan over medium heat until melted and nut-brown, then add the leeks and sauté for 6–8 minutes or until softened and just tender. Season with salt and pepper to taste and set aside.

- Blanch asparagus in a saucepan of boiling salted water. Slice into 2 cm lengths and add to leeks with the parsley.

- Whisk egg yolks, then add cream and a little salt and pepper and whisk to combine.

- Scatter asparagus and leek mixture over the tart shell, then pour over egg yolk and cream mixture and top with grated Parmigiano Reggiano.

- Bake tart for 45–60 minutes or until the custard sets. Cool for about 10 minutes, then serve with a green salad alongside.

Chook Legs with Vino Cotto or Balsamic

8 Barossa or other corn-fed chicken marylands (thigh and leg joints), thighs and legs separated

zest of 2 lemons, removed in wide strips with a vegetable peeler (reserve flesh for squeezing before serving)

5 fresh bay leaves

2 stalks rosemary

¼ stick cinnamon, ground or ½ teaspoon ground cinnamon

extra virgin olive oil, for drizzling

½ cup flaked almonds

40 g unsalted butter

sea salt

¼ cup vino cotto or balsamic vinegar

16 green olives

½ cup raisins

¼ cup salted capers, rinsed and drained

chopped flat-leaf parsley, to serve

SERVES 8

Given that my daughter Saskia produces such well brought-up chooks, I always have ready access to high-quality chicken. So it is that I often turn to chicken when looking for something to cook for a crowd. I find chook legs to be especially suited to this purpose as no last minute carving is required. This dish has the added benefit of being able to be served in its cooking pot. This is also fantastic served cold the next day, when the pan juices become jellied.

Sometimes I use caperberries instead of capers, but they can be a bit vinegary so use less and soak them in cold water first.

- Marinate chicken with lemon zest, bay leaves, rosemary, cinnamon and a good splash of extra virgin olive oil for at least 1 hour before cooking; overnight is even better if you have the time.

- Preheat fan-forced oven to 180°C (350°F).

- Place flaked almonds on a baking tray and roast for 5 minutes or until golden, then set aside to cool. Increase oven temperature to 200°C (400°F).

- Heat butter in a large ovenproof frying pan over medium heat. Season chicken with salt, then remove from the marinade. Working in batches so you don't crowd the pan, gently pan-fry chicken pieces for 8–10 minutes or until golden brown all over. Transfer pan to the oven and roast chicken for 10 minutes.

- Deglaze pan with vino cotto or balsamic over high heat, then add olives, raisins and capers. Return to oven for another 10 minutes or until the chicken is cooked through.

- Toss over almonds and parsley, then squeeze over the juice of at least one of the reserved lemons, taste and add more lemon juice, if needed.

- Leave to rest for 10 minutes, then serve.

Mussels in Tomato Sugo

2 cups tomato passata or homemade
Tomato Sugo (see recipe page 167)

1 cup verjuice or dry white wine

1 kg black mussels, cleaned and bearded

extra virgin olive oil, basil leaves and
crusty bread, to serve

SERVES 4

Mussels are definitely an under-rated ingredient. They are so full of flavour and inexpensive to boot; the trick is not to overcook them. I recommend cooking this dish in a wide, deep frying pan with a tight-fitting lid – a glass lid is ideal as you can see when each mussel opens and remove them as they do. For some reason, there can be a good five minute gap between when the first and last mussels open, and you don't want to overcook them.

Make sure you have a supply of good extra virgin olive oil to hand for dousing the mussels just before serving, plus some fresh crusty bread to sop up all the delicious juices.

- Combine tomato passata and verjuice or white wine in a deep, wide frying pan. Cover and bring to the boil over high heat. Simmer until slightly reduced and thickened. Add cleaned mussels, cover again and bring back to the boil, then cook until mussels have opened. Take each mussel out the moment it opens. Remove and discard any unopened mussels as they may be off.
- Drizzle mussels with olive oil, then scatter with torn basil. Serve with crusty bread to the side.

Char-grilled Lamb

1 × 1.4 kg boned and butterflied
leg of lamb (I use Richard Gunner's
Pure Suffolk Lamb), cut into 4 pieces
(ask your butcher to do this)

6 stalks rosemary, leaves picked

4 stalks thyme, leaves picked

2 cloves garlic, crushed

extra virgin olive oil, for cooking

sea salt

¼ cup verjuice

¼ cup chopped flat-leaf parsley
(optional)

¼ cup kalamata olives, pitted

SERVES 6-8

The use of a post-cooking marinade is one worth trying with many foods cooked on the barbecue as it adds so much moisture – it could be as simple as placing lots of fresh rosemary, thyme or bay leaves in extra virgin olive oil with a splash of verjuice.

Using a good-quality cut of lamb from an heirloom breed such as Suffolk will make a huge difference to the texture and flavour of such a simple dish.

It's important to carve the lamb (or any other meat) against the grain and to always use a sharp knife so you don't tear the meat.

- Flatten and trim lamb pieces to make sure they are of equal thickness (this helps them to cook evenly). Chop rosemary, thyme and garlic together, then add enough olive oil to form a thick paste. Massage herb paste into lamb, then leave to marinate at room temperature for 1 hour.
- Heat a barbecue char-grill plate as hot as possible. Season lamb with salt and drizzle with more olive oil, then place, skin-side down on the barbecue for 2-3 minutes or until skin is caramelised. Season lamb with salt and turn over, then reduce heat to low and cook, covered, for another 7 minutes for medium-rare, or continue until cooked to your liking, checking and turning several times to ensure it doesn't burn. If your barbecue doesn't have a hood, then move lamb to the coolest part of the grill plate. (If your lamb pieces are very thick, then after browning on the barbecue cook in a pre-heated 200°C (400°F) fan-forced oven for 12 minutes instead.)
- Transfer lamb to a dish, then add ⅓ cup olive oil, verjuice, parsley, if using, and olives and leave to rest, covered loosely with foil, for 15-20 minutes. (If kept near a warm stove lamb will retain its temperature during this time.)
- Carve lamb into thick slices, then spoon over some of the olive and parsley mixture and serve.

Spatchcock in a Fig 'Bath'

4 × 500 g spatchcock

180 g unsalted butter, at room temperature, chopped

1 tablespoon finely chopped rosemary

2 teaspoons finely chopped thyme

2 teaspoons finely grated lemon zest

sea salt and freshly ground black pepper

FIG 'BATH'

6 very ripe figs, halved or 10 small dried Persian figs, halved lengthways

verjuice or water (optional), for soaking

4 stalks rosemary, leaves picked

6 wide strips lemon zest removed with a vegetable peeler, plus juice of 1 lemon

⅓ cup extra virgin olive oil

sea salt and freshly ground black pepper

SERVES 4

You might see young chickens sold labelled either as spatchcocks or poussins – whichever name is used, the great advantage of cooking them is that they are generally a suitable size to serve one adult (or two children). The term 'spatchcock' also refers to the process of removing the backbone, then flattening out the bird so it cooks more quickly. I like to barbecue spatchcock, then let them rest in a post-cooking marinade such as this fig 'bath' so they soak up the juices; I find they can be a little dry if served directly from being cooked over high heat on the barbecue.

Whilst it is not essential, an added touch is to quickly char-grill the fresh or reconstituted figs after first brushing them with olive oil (see opposite).

* Place a spatchcock, breast-side down, on a chopping board and cut along both sides of the backbone with sharp poultry shears. Remove backbone, then turn spatchcock over and gently press breast with the palm of your hand to flatten. Repeat with remaining spatchcock.

* Combine butter, rosemary, thyme and lemon zest. Using your fingers, gently ease skin away from breasts, then rub one-quarter of the butter mixture between the skin and breasts of each spatchcock. With buttery hands, rub any leftover butter mixture over skin of the birds, then season well with salt.

* Heat a char-grill pan over high heat until very hot. Working in batches, if necessary, cook spatchcock on both sides until golden all over, moving them around the pan and turning so that the legs cook without drying out the breasts. After 7–8 minutes (about halfway through cooking), cover spatch-cock with a saucepan or stainless steel bowl to create a mini-oven so that they cook all the way through. This should take about 15 minutes in total, depending on the size of each bird.

* Meanwhile, for the fig 'bath', if using dried figs then soak them in verjuice or water until reconstituted then drain. Place soaked or fresh figs, rosemary, lemon zest and juice and olive oil in a shallow dish large enough to accommodate the spatchcock in one layer, then season with salt and pepper.

* Transfer cooked spatchcock to the fig 'bath', breast-sides down, and leave to rest for 10 minutes. Turn spatchcock over so they are breast-sides up before serving.

* Serve spatchcock with some of the fig 'bath' juices and figs spooned over as a dressing.

Camel Scotch Fillet Marinated in Lilly Pilly

finely grated zest of ½ orange

1 heaped tablespoon juniper berries

6-8 unsprayed lilly pilly leaves
or fresh bay leaves, crumpled

3-4 cloves garlic, thinly sliced

freshly ground black pepper

4 × 200 g thick camel scotch fillet
or sirloin steaks

extra virgin olive oil, for drizzling

sea salt

rocket leaves (optional), to serve

HONEY DATE RELISH

extra virgin olive oil, for cooking

2 golden shallots, thinly sliced

200 g honey dates or other fresh
dates, halved and stoned

½ cup white balsamic vinegar

juice of 3 oranges, plus 1 teaspoon
finely grated orange zest

1 large fresh bay leaf

1 stick cinnamon

sea salt and freshly ground black pepper

SERVES 4

I recently visited Alice Springs for the first time, to judge the Wild Bush Foods Recipe Competition that was part of the Alice Desert Festival, and it was a really fascinating experience. I loved the Alice, and the energy and enthusiasm of the local amateur cooks who entered the competition was nothing short of thrilling. A visit to Alice Springs Desert Park, with two wonderful Aboriginal women as my guides, was somewhat of an epiphany for me – the park was so full of beauty and bounty that I will never think the same way about the desert again.

In conjunction with the festival, there was a competition in the town for the best camel recipe – it was the first time I had tried camel and I found it to be really good. It's well worth trying, especially if you can get a thick piece of scotch fillet with a little fat still attached, otherwise use the sirloin instead. If you can get fresh lilly pilly berries, then use those in place of the juniper.

♦ For the honey date relish, heat a splash of olive oil in a small saucepan over medium heat, then sauté shallots for 5 minutes. Add dates and cook for a couple of minutes. Deglaze the pan with white balsamic and continue cooking for another 5 minutes or until a little syrupy. Add half of the orange juice and continue to cook over low heat for 10-15 minutes or until the dates have absorbed the juice, then add the orange zest, bay leaf, cinnamon and remaining orange juice so that the mixture is thick but rich and moist at the same time. Remove from the heat and set aside to infuse until needed (or pour into a sterilised jar and seal for use later). Just before serving the relish, remove the cinnamon stick, adjust the seasoning with salt and pepper to taste and add another splash of olive oil.

♦ Place orange zest, juniper berries, lilly pilly or bay leaves, garlic and pepper in a mortar and crush with a pestle until you can smell their essential oils and the ingredients look bruised but not pounded.

♦ Pat steaks dry with paper towels and place in a dish large enough to hold them snugly, top with lilly pilly mixture, then pour olive oil over the steaks. Marinate camel in the refrigerator for a few hours or overnight if possible.

♦ Remove camel steaks from the refrigerator at least 1 hour before you plan to cook them. Scrape the excess marinade from the meat and season with sea salt.

♦ Heat a char-grill pan or barbecue grill-plate until as hot as possible, then cook camel steaks for a couple of minutes on each side for medium-rare or until cooked to your liking. Drizzle with oil, then leave to rest for a few minutes.

♦ Serve camel steaks with rocket leaves, if desired, and small bowls of honey date relish to the side.

Soft Polenta with Sautéed Mushrooms

2¾ cups milk, plus extra, as needed

2 cups water

1 fresh bay leaf

1 cup fine polenta

1½ teaspoons sea salt

freshly ground black pepper

40 g unsalted butter, plus extra
for cooking

⅔ cup mascarpone

100 g grated pecorino, plus extra to serve

extra virgin olive oil, for cooking

3 cloves garlic, finely chopped

500 g large mushrooms (such as
portobello), thickly sliced

2 tablespoons thyme, roughly chopped

2 teaspoons lemon thyme,
roughly chopped

¼ cup verjuice

SERVES 6

There is something very comforting about serving a large bowl or platter of soft polenta in the centre of your table. Cooked this way, polenta has the consistency of porridge – maybe that's why I find it so soothing. The earthy flavour of the sautéed mushrooms is a great counterpoint to the creaminess of the polenta. You could also try serving the polenta with good pork sausages and caramelised onions as a change from mash or use Parmigiano Reggiano or goat's curd instead of pecorino for a different flavour altogether.

• Bring the milk, water and bay leaf to the boil over high heat, then remove from the heat and leave to infuse for 20 minutes.

• Strain milk mixture into a heavy-based saucepan, discarding bay leaf, then bring to the boil again. Slowly pour in the polenta, add salt and stir continuously over low heat for 20-25 minutes or until it thickens and comes away from the side of the pan; the exact cooking time will depend on the brand. If in doubt, taste to check, as undercooked polenta is most unappetising. Stir in butter, mascarpone and grated pecorino until well combined, then season with salt and pepper if necessary. The polenta should be soft and creamy – you want a sloppy, porridge-like consistency, so you may need to add a little extra milk to loosen it if it becomes too stiff.

• Melt a large knob of butter with a splash of olive oil in a large non-stick frying pan over medium-high heat. When butter starts bubbling, add garlic. Working in batches so you don't crowd the pan, and adding butter and olive oil as necessary, sauté mushrooms with a little of the herbs for a few minutes or until golden and just tender; they should still be lovely and moist. Season with salt and pepper and deglaze the pan with verjuice.

• Pour soft polenta into a serving dish, then top with sautéed mushrooms and pecorino and serve.

Moroccan Ocean Trout

¼ cup pine nuts

¼ cup rose tea leaves (available from specialty tea stores or substitute with rosehip tea with a handful of unsprayed rose petals added)

1 cup boiling water

extra virgin olive oil, for cooking

2 golden shallots, very thinly sliced

1 tablespoon dried currants

1 tablespoon sultanas

juice of 1 large lemon

1 teaspoon caster sugar

4 wide strips orange zest, removed with a potato peeler

3 teaspoons ras el hanout (Moroccan spice blend available from specialty food stores) or ground cinnamon

⅓ cup plain flour

sea salt and freshly ground black pepper

4 × 160 g ocean trout or salmon fillets, skin removed and pin-boned

unsprayed rose petals and thinly sliced mint (optional), to serve

SERVES 4

This dish is not only delicious but it is also really pretty, if that is important to you. It features ras el hanout, a spice blend I've become converted to since a recent trip to Morocco, where I was advised that it is the very best of all Moroccan spice mixes. Containing up to twenty different spices, all mixed to form a subtle, but balanced blend, ras el hanout loosely translates as 'top of the shop', as traditionally each spice shop makes its own mix. I witnessed the most amazing kaleidoscope of colour when I visited a spice shop in the souk in Marrakesh (not to mention some of the best 'sales patter' as well), so I ended up bringing a bag home – duly declared of course. Since it ran out I've been delighted to find that Ian Hemphill of Herbie's Spices (herbies.com.au) sells his own special blend by mail order.

- Preheat fan-forced oven to 180°C (350°F).
- Place pine nuts on a baking tray and roast for 5 minutes or until golden. Set aside.
- Combine rose tea with boiling water and set aside to steep for 5 minutes.
- Heat a splash of olive oil in a saucepan over medium heat, then fry shallots for 5-7 minutes or until translucent. Strain tea, then pour half over the currants and sultanas and leave them to plump. Pour the other half over the shallots. Add currants, sultanas, lemon juice, sugar and orange rind to shallot mixture and bring to the boil. Simmer over low heat for 3 minutes.
- Mix ras el hanout with flour and season with salt and pepper. Heat a splash of olive oil in a frying pan over medium heat, then lightly dust fish with flour mixture, shaking to remove excess. Cook fish fillets briefly in the frying pan on both sides until golden, then transfer to a baking dish. Pour over the rose tea liquid and bake fish for 4-6 minutes or until cooked through (the exact time will depend on the thickness of the fillets).
- Divide fish between 4 plates, then spoon a little poaching liquid over and scatter with roasted pine nuts. Drizzle with olive oil and finish off with rose petals and mint, if you like and serve immediately.

Chicken, Grape and Champagne Pies

40 g unsalted butter

extra virgin olive oil, for cooking

3-4 large chicken thigh fillets with skin-on (about 770 g), cut into 1.5 cm pieces

sea salt

2 leeks, white parts only, cleaned and thinly sliced

2 cloves garlic, finely chopped

1 cup Champagne or sparkling white wine

¼ cup plain flour

1½ cups chicken stock (preferably homemade)

1½ tablespoons finely chopped French tarragon

1½ tablespoons finely chopped thyme

½ preserved lemon, flesh removed, rind rinsed and finely chopped

2 tablespoons verjuice

freshly ground black pepper

225 g seedless green grapes (1 cup picked grapes)

1 quantity Sour-cream Pastry (see recipe page 92)

olive oil spray, for greasing

1 free-range egg, lightly beaten

rocket leaves, to serve

MAKES 4 INDIVIDUAL PIES
OR 1 LARGE PIE

What is it about pies that I find so appealing? Firstly, it's about using a great pastry (that's a given) and then it's having a filling that transforms them from being a snack food into something worthy of serving as a great meal. Pies are so self-contained that they make perfect dinner fare for when you want to invite a group of friends and are looking for something that just needs to be served with a beautiful salad or lovely steamed seasonal greens alongside.

Here I took advantage of the seasons and used some of my autumn bounty of fresh grapes, but at other times you could replace them with half the amount of sultanas reconstituted in a little of the Champagne.

This pastry is quite buttery so it needs a quick burst of high heat when you start cooking the pies in order to stop it from being soggy.

- Heat butter in a large frying pan over high heat until nut-brown, then add a splash of olive oil. Season chicken with salt, then sauté in batches until lightly coloured. Remove from pan and set aside.

- Add leeks and garlic to the pan and cook over low heat for 5 minutes or until soft. Increase heat to high, then deglaze pan with Champagne or sparkling white wine and cook over medium heat for 2 minutes or until wine has reduced by half. Sprinkle in flour and whisk in well to combine, then add stock and bring to the simmer. Add chicken, tarragon, thyme and preserved lemon, stirring gently to combine, then cook for 4-5 minutes. Add verjuice and simmer for another 2-3 minutes. Season with pepper and add salt if needed. Remove chicken from heat, then add grapes and leave mixture to cool completely.

- Meanwhile, make sour-cream pastry according to instructions on page 92.

- Grease four 10 cm × 7 cm pie tins with olive oil spray (or you could use 1 large pie tin). Roll out pastry until 3 mm thick, then cut out four 19 cm rounds for the pie bases and four 12 cm rounds for the lids. Line each pie tin with a 19 cm round, then divide the cooled chicken filling among the tins. Wet pastry edges with a little water and top with pastry lids. Press pastry edges together to seal, then trim away any excess with a small sharp knife. Pierce a small hole in the centre of each pie top, then brush the pastry with a little beaten egg.

- Place pies in the refrigerator to chill the pastry for at least 20 minutes before baking.

- Preheat fan-forced oven to 220°C (450°F).

- Bake pies for 25-30 minutes or until pastry is golden. Remove from oven and leave to cool slightly before turning out and serving with rocket leaves to the side.

Roast Barossa Chook with Preserved Lemon and Tarragon Butter

125 g unsalted butter, softened and chopped

2 small quarters preserved lemon, flesh removed, rind rinsed and finely chopped

⅓ cup French tarragon leaves

1 × 2 kg Barossa or other well brought-up chook

2 cloves garlic, crushed

sea salt and freshly ground black pepper

2 tablespoons extra virgin olive oil

½ cup verjuice

SERVES 4-6

This recipe definitely falls into the realm of Beer family comfort food, served as often for friends as it is for family. Whenever I'm in doubt of what to cook I roast a beautiful Barossa chook stuffed under the skin with this mix of preserved lemon and tarragon butter. These well brought-up chooks are so rich in flavour and texture that, when cooking them, they are just about invincible. Leave the chook to rest upside down for a long period before serving, so that its lovely juices flow into the breast to keep it moist; it will remain hot for a good thirty minutes.

- Preheat fan-forced oven to 170°C (340°F).

- Place butter, preserved lemon and tarragon in a food processor and whiz to combine; don't over-process or the butter will split.

- Place chook, breast-side up, in a shallow roasting pan and use your hands to separate the skin from the flesh, working from the legs then up and across both breasts. Tuck the wings underneath the chicken. Place garlic in the cavity. Push butter mixture under the skin with your fingertips. Season chicken with salt and pepper and rub olive oil into the skin.

- Roast for 40 minutes. Pour verjuice over the chook and return to the oven for another 10 minutes or until chicken is cooked through. Check by inserting a skewer through the thickest part of the thigh joint to make sure the juices run clear. If there are any signs of pinkness, return to the oven. If you have a meat thermometer it should read 68°C (155°F) when inserted into this joint.

- Leave the cooked chicken to stand, breast-side down in the roasting juices, in a warm place for at least 20 minutes before carving.

Skate with Olives and Preserved Lemon

2 × 200 g skate fillets, skin removed

plain flour, for dusting

sea salt and freshly ground black pepper

60 g unsalted butter, chopped

extra virgin olive oil, for cooking

juice of 1 lemon

1 quarter preserved lemon, flesh removed, rind rinsed and thinly sliced

6 green olives, sliced from the stones

¼ cup flat-leaf parsley, roughly chopped

SERVES 2

I've found that skate is prepared and sold differently in each of the states. It's much easier if you can buy it already skinned, but in South Australia this is often not the case. I always request smaller skate, with the skin and cartilage removed. The key to this dish is lightly dusting the skate with flour, then pan-frying it in nut-brown butter, deglazing the pan with lemon juice and throwing in some chopped flat-leaf parsley. Here I've add preserved lemon and olives – all flavours that go together – but I could just as easily have kept it simple by just tossing in some capers with the parsley instead.

- Dust skate fillets with flour seasoned with salt and pepper, shaking to remove excess. Heat butter and a splash of olive oil in a frying pan over medium heat until butter turns nut-brown. Add skate fillets and cook for 1 minute on each side, then deglaze pan with lemon juice and transfer skate to 2 plates.

- Add preserved lemon and olives to the pan and immediately remove from the heat, then add parsley. Season to taste with salt and pepper.

- Pour preserved lemon and olive sauce over the skate, then serve immediately.

Kingfish with Roasted Tomatoes, Capers and Olives

8 small vine-ripened tomatoes, halved lengthways

sea salt and freshly ground black pepper

2 teaspoons thyme, roughly chopped

extra virgin olive oil, for cooking

40 g unsalted butter

plain flour, for dusting

4 × 160 g kingfish fillets, skin-on and pin-boned

⅓ cup large green olives, pitted and halved

⅓ cup salted capers, rinsed or 6 caperberriers, halved widthways

2 tablespoons marjoram leaves, plus extra to serve

½ cup flat-leaf parsley leaves (optional)

squeeze of lemon juice

SERVES 4

The Hiramasa kingfish is a great example of a farmed fish. When I can get hold of it super-fresh I particularly like to serve it raw, simply drizzled with some top-notch extra virgin olive oil, scattered with chopped herbs and a final flourish of lemon or lime juice just before serving. Like barramundi, it is a very dense-fleshed fish, so when pan-frying fillets you need to sear and colour them on both sides, then manoeuvre them around the pan so the thickest parts cook through without overcooking the thinner parts.

If you haven't time to roast the tomatoes, just toss some salted capers into the pan with the nut-brown butter, add loads of chopped flat-leaf parsley, then serve the fish with a good squeeze of lemon juice.

+ Preheat fan-forced oven to 150°C (300°F).

+ Place tomatoes, cut-sides up, on a baking tray lined with baking paper. Season with salt and pepper, sprinkle with thyme and drizzle with olive oil, then roast for 1-4 hours or until tomatoes are soft but still retain their shape (the exact time will depend on variety and ripeness of your tomatoes). Leave to cool.

+ Melt butter with a splash of olive oil in a frying pan over medium heat. Dust kingfish with flour seasoned with salt and pepper, then place skin-sides down in the pan and cook for 4-5 minutes on each side or until cooked through, turning once only.

+ Heat a generous splash of olive oil in another frying pan over low heat, then add olives, capers or caperberries and marjoram and cook for 5 minutes. Remove from heat and set aside for flavours to infuse.

+ Combine roasted tomatoes with olive and caper mixture, then add flat-leaf parsley, if using, and a squeeze of lemon juice.

+ Divide kingfish and roasted tomato mixture between 4 plates, then scatter with marjoram leaves, drizzle with olive oil and serve immediately.

My Spag Bog

extra virgin olive oil, for cooking

1 small onion, roughly chopped

2 cloves garlic, crushed

200 g chicken livers

2 tablespoons finely chopped oregano

500 g minced beef

sea salt

500 g minced pork

280 g tomato paste

300 ml red wine

½ cup chicken, beef or vegetable stock

2 tablespoons finely chopped thyme

2 small fresh bay leaves

500 g dried spaghetti

freshly ground black pepper

chopped flat-leaf parsley, to serve

SERVES 6

Whilst you don't have to follow my lead and add chicken livers to your spaghetti bolognese, they're the jewel in the crown for me. The trick to cooking this is to sauté the meat in batches so that each batch is really well browned. To me, the addition of red wine is essential as it really adds another level of richness. I've given 20 to 25 minutes as the total cooking time, but the real test as to whether it is ready is the colour – the amalgamation of the meat, tomato paste and red wine should lead to a deep, richly coloured result.

♦ Heat a splash of olive oil in a saucepan over medium heat and sauté onion and garlic for 10 minutes or until translucent, then add oregano. Transfer to a bowl and set aside. Add livers to the pan and cook for 30 seconds on both sides or until coloured, then remove and leave to cool. Remove connective tissue, then cut livers into pieces and set aside.

♦ Add another splash of olive oil to the pan and add minced beef in batches, then season with salt and sauté until browned. Add minced pork in batches and cook until browned. Return onion mixture to pan, then add tomato paste and cook over low heat for 10 minutes. Add wine, stock, thyme and bay leaves, then bring to a simmer and cook for 20-25 minutes or longer if needed. Add livers to bolognese mixture 5 minutes before serving.

♦ Meanwhile, cook spaghetti in a large saucepan of boiling salted water according to manufacturers' instructions, and have warm plates or bowls ready to serve.

♦ Season bolognese with pepper, then serve with drained spaghetti and generous amounts of chopped parsley.

Barbecued Quail

6 quail

¼ cup wholegrain mustard

½ cup honey

2 tablespoons extra virgin olive oil,
plus extra for cooking

2 tablespoons finely chopped rosemary

2 tablespoons lemon juice,
plus extra to serve

sea salt

SERVES 4

Quail is one of my favourite foods, especially whole quail, as much of my delight in eating them comes from using my fingers and chewing on the bones. The best quail I've ever eaten came from Game Farm in New South Wales – they sell 'jumbo' quail that are much plumper than the average quail, so remain beautifully moist after cooking. I often find that serving one quail per person is not sufficient, unless I've cooked it with a generous stuffing (see the recipe for Quince-glazed Quail on page 173), so I generally cook a few extra, cut them in half and then give guests the choice as to how many pieces they would like.

I need to declare that adding honey to the marinade makes the quail burn more easily, so take care when cooking – whilst caramelised is perfect, burnt is not!

My principle of leaving barbecued foods to rest in a post-cooking marinade or 'bath' works beautifully here – try the fig one I've used with spatchcock on page 98 (see opposite).

- To butterfly the quail, cut along either sides of the backbones, removing the spines, then press down to flatten the birds with the palm of your hand. Tuck the wings in behind. Otherwise, ask your butcher to do this for you.

- Mix the mustard, honey, olive oil and rosemary together and use to marinate the butterflied quail for at least 1 hour. Add lemon juice just before cooking, otherwise it will start to 'cook' the quail.

- Season quail with a little salt, then wipe a barbecue grill-plate and flat-plate with a little olive oil and heat until hot. Place quail, skin-side down, onto the hot grill-plate and leave to sear. Take care not to turn before the quail have seared because this will tear the skin, but also be careful not to burn the honey. As soon as the quail are seared, turn and sear on the other sides. Transfer to the hot flat-plate and cook, skin-side up, for about 4 minutes or until cooked through, taking care not to let the birds dry out.

- Drizzle the quail with a little olive oil and add a squeeze of lemon juice and leave to rest, skin-side down, in a warm place, then serve.

Crisp-skin Salmon with Pea Salsa

4 × 140 g salmon steaks, skin-on

sea salt

extra virgin olive oil, for drizzling

10 g unsalted butter

juice of 1 lemon

chervil sprigs and lemon wedges, to serve

FROZEN PEA SALSA

30 g unsalted butter

extra virgin olive oil, for cooking

2 golden shallots, finely chopped

¾ cup chicken stock

1½ cups frozen peas

1 sprig chervil

sea salt and freshly ground black pepper

SERVES 4

This is definitely my idea of fast food. I keep individual salmon fillets with the skin-on wrapped separately in the freezer for those days when I've not organised anything for dinner in advance. The fat content in salmon means it freezes well – I've even roasted it in the oven straight from the freezer if I've forgotten to take it out to thaw. Of course, you need to use super-fresh fillets which you are sure haven't already been frozen to start with so that they still taste fresh after thawing. Given my hectic schedule these days, there are times when Colin and I will eat crisp-skin salmon with either this pea salsa or seasonal greens from my garden for dinner at least once, if not more, every week.

For a quick mid-week meal, I often do nothing more than pan-fry salmon fillets, skin side-down and with a good dose of sea salt, until almost cooked, then serve them with a drizzle of extra virgin olive oil, squeeze of lemon juice or splash of verjuice and a grinding of freshly ground black pepper, with zucchini freshly picked from my garden during summer or a salad at any time of the year (I just vary the leaves depending on what is in season).

The pea salsa is another one of those fantastic kitchen standbys I can prepare at the drop of a hat when I haven't planned on making anything else.

- For the frozen pea salsa, melt butter in a deep frying pan with a little olive oil over medium heat, then add shallots and sauté for 10 minutes or until translucent.

- Meanwhile, bring chicken stock to the boil in another saucepan. Add peas and chervil to the shallots, then, when the peas have thawed, add the hot chicken stock and bring to the boil. Remove from the heat and leave to cool slightly. Purée the pea mixture in a blender (or use a mouli if you have one), then season with salt and pepper, if you like.

- Heat a large frying pan over medium heat. Season skin-sides of the salmon steaks with salt. Add a splash of olive oil to the hot pan, then cook the salmon steaks, skin-sides down, for 2 minutes or until the skin is crisp and you can see from the side that they are cooked at least halfway through.

- Season the other side of the fish with salt, then quickly wipe the pan with paper towel, drop in the butter, and, when melted, gently turn the salmon over, using either a palette knife or spatula. Immediately remove the pan from the heat, then leave salmon steaks to sit in the hot pan for 5 minutes. The centre of the fish should be just set or a little rare.

- Place a salmon steak on each plate, then top each with a spoonful of pea salsa. Squeeze over the lemon juice, sprinkle with chervil and drizzle with a little olive oil, then serve with lemon wedges to the side.

Radicchio Risotto

½ cup walnuts

1.5 litres chicken or vegetable stock

120 g unsalted butter, chopped

⅓ cup extra virgin olive oil

1 large onion, finely chopped

1 tablespoon finely chopped lemon thyme

finely grated zest of 1 lemon, plus lemon juice to serve

750 g radicchio, leaves separated, washed and cut into 5 mm thick slices (about 2 large radicchio)

2 cups risotto rice (such as superfino carnaroli, see page 27)

½ cup verjuice or dry white wine

sea salt

60 g grated Parmigano Reggiano

freshly ground black pepper

125 g gorgonzola, chopped

chopped flat-leaf parsley, to serve

SERVES 4-6

I'm a real fan of radicchio, whether it is raw in salads, halved lengthways and braised in butter until almost cooked and then deglazed with vino cotto, or featured as the star ingredient in a risotto, as I've done here. I love the balance to its bitterness provided by the equally intense flavour of a great local blue cheese or even gorgonzola, but Persian feta would work too. The addition of roasted walnuts just before serving provides both crunch and flavour – and don't forget to add the squeeze of lemon juice and freshly ground black pepper before you serve.

- Preheat fan-forced oven to 180°C (350°F). Place walnuts on a baking tray and roast for 10 minutes, checking frequently to make sure they don't burn. Immediately wrap in a clean tea towel, then rub to peel off skins. Sift rubbed walnuts through a sieve to get rid of skins, then leave to cool.

- Bring stock to the boil in a saucepan. Keep warm.

- Heat butter and olive oil in a heavy-based saucepan or deep frying pan over low heat, then sauté onion for 10 minutes or until golden. Add thyme and lemon zest and cook so that their flavour is absorbed by the onion. Add radicchio and toss to coat in onion mixture, then cook for a few minutes or until wilted. You may need to add a little more butter as there also needs to be enough to coat the rice. Add rice and stir to coat, then increase heat to high and deglaze the pan with verjuice. Reduce heat to low and cook until verjuice evaporates. Season with salt.

- Add hot stock to rice mixture, a ladleful at a time, stirring continuously and waiting for each addition to be absorbed before adding the next. Continue for about 20 minutes or until all the stock has been absorbed and the rice is cooked but still a little firm; it should not be chalky in the centre. The last ladleful of stock might not be used, depending on whether you like your risotto thick and creamy or slightly soupy.

- Remove pan from the heat, then stir in Parmigiano. Season to taste with salt and pepper, then add gorgonzola immediately before serving.

- Scatter with chopped parsley and walnuts, if using, then serve bowls of risotto with a squeeze of lemon juice added.

Lamb Moussaka

extra virgin olive oil, for cooking

1 onion, finely chopped

1 clove garlic, crushed

500 g minced lamb

1 × 1 cm piece cinnamon stick, pounded

sea salt

½ cup red wine

1 tablespoon tomato paste

1 cup Tomato Sugo (see recipe page 167) or tomato passata

2 tablespoons chopped lemon thyme

finely grated zest of 1 lemon

3 medium-sized eggplants (aubergines), cut into 1.5–2 cm thick slices

sea salt

BÉCHAMEL SAUCE

50 g unsalted butter

50 g plain flour

1 cup milk (full-cream is best)

1 cup chicken stock

pinch of freshly grated or ground nutmeg

sea salt and freshly ground white pepper

2 tablespoons grated Parmigiano Reggiano

CRUST

¼ cup grated Parmigiano Reggiano

¼ cup fresh breadcrumbs

2 teaspoons finely chopped lemon thyme

1 tablespoon rinsed and finely chopped preserved lemon rind

SERVES 6

My friend Peter Wall often cooks dinner for us, especially on the frequent occasions when I've been travelling and arrive home jetlagged. I always love his moussaka – it is lighter than any other I'd ever eaten so I coaxed the recipe from him, which was happily given. Peter's secret is to use a really good chicken stock in the béchamel sauce. Starting from this, I added my favourite bits from my vegetarian moussaka and the result is this recipe.

• Heat a splash of olive oil in a large saucepan over low heat and sauté onion for 5 minutes, then add garlic and cook for another 5 minutes. Push onion and garlic to one side of the pan, then brown lamb with cinnamon in batches over high heat and season with salt. Return all meat to the pan, add wine, tomato paste and tomato sugo, then stir to combine and bring to the boil. Add lemon thyme and lemon zest and simmer over low heat for 20 minutes.

• Meanwhile, for the béchamel sauce, melt butter in a saucepan over medium heat. Sprinkle over flour, stirring well to combine, then cook for another few minutes or until flour colours slightly. Remove from the heat and slowly pour in milk and then stock, whisking continuously to prevent any lumps forming. Return to the heat and stir with a wooden spoon for another 10 minutes or until the sauce thickens and coats the back of the spoon. Add nutmeg, then season to taste with salt and pepper and stir in Parmigiano Reggiano. Cover the surface of the sauce closely with plastic film to stop a skin from forming and set aside until needed.

• Brush eggplant with olive oil, then cook on a hot char-grill pan over high heat until golden on both sides.

• Preheat fan-forced oven to 200°C (400°F).

• Lightly grease a 1 litre baking dish with olive oil. Place a layer of eggplant in the base of the dish, then a layer of lamb mixture, and repeating the layering process until all the eggplant and lamb mixture are used, finishing with a layer of eggplant. Pour the béchamel sauce over the eggplant.

• For the crust, mix together all the ingredients and generously sprinkle the mixture over béchamel. (This dish can be frozen at this stage, then baked later.)

• Bake lamb moussaka for 30 minutes or until the top is golden. Serve at once.

Honey and Lemon Chicken Drummettes

½ cup honey, warmed

1 tablespoon roughly chopped lemon thyme, plus extra to serve (optional)

¼ cup extra virgin olive oil

1 tablespoon finely grated lemon zest

⅓ cup lemon juice

1 kg chicken drummettes

sea salt

SERVES 4-6

Whilst I love making this dish with my grandchildren, this doesn't mean that I see it just as a 'children's meal' – I've never known any adults to refuse these tasty little morsels. Although I usually bake them, the drummettes could be cooked on a barbecue too; however, you'd need to turn the chicken frequently to prevent the honey in the marinade from burning. Don't forget to leave the drummettes to rest a little before serving – not only does this make them easier to pick up, but it maximises their flavour and moistness.

Chicken drummettes are the small drumsticks attached to the wing bones. If you are unable to buy them separately, then buy whole wings instead (with the wing tips removed) and cut them in two at the joint.

- Mix honey, thyme, olive oil, lemon zest and lemon juice together, then use to marinate the drummettes in the refrigerator for 20 minutes.
- Preheat fan-forced oven to 220°C (450°F).
- Season chicken drummettes with salt, then place on a baking tray in one layer and bake for 15 minutes or until cooked through, turning halfway through cooking.
- Leave chicken drummettes to rest for 5 minutes, then serve scattered with extra lemon thyme leaves, if desired.

Herb-crusted Flathead

1 plump bulb fennel, trimmed and sliced lengthways

4 ripe roma tomatoes, thickly sliced

sea salt and freshly ground black pepper

½ cup verjuice

extra virgin olive oil, for cooking

½ cup chopped flat-leaf parsley

¼ cup chopped mixed herbs such as oregano, thyme and fennel fronds

1 teaspoon finely grated lemon zest

2 tablespoons salted capers, rinsed

½ preserved lemon, flesh removed, rind rinsed and finely chopped

40 g unsalted butter, at room temperature

2 cups fresh breadcrumbs

4 × 160 g flathead fillets, skin removed and pin-boned

lemon wedges, to serve

SERVES 4

I love the sweet flavour of fresh flathead – it's a real favourite of mine so I seek it out whenever I can. I think the best possible way of experiencing flathead is to pan-fry it whole over low heat in lots of melted nut-brown butter and a splash of extra virgin olive oil and seasoned with sea salt and freshly ground black pepper, with either a squeeze of lemon juice or splash of verjuice to finish the dish. However, I've come to accept that so many people are put off eating fish because of the bones, and have found that cooking fillets like this is a way to convert otherwise reluctant fish eaters. The herb crust keeps the fish beautifully moist, and the roasted tomatoes and fennel make it a complete meal.

- Preheat fan-forced oven to 200°C (400°F).
- Place fennel and tomatoes in a baking dish, then season with salt and pepper. Add verjuice and drizzle with olive oil, then roast for about 10 minutes or until fennel starts to cook.
- Meanwhile, pulse herbs, lemon zest, capers, preserved lemon, butter, breadcrumbs and 2 tablespoons olive oil in a food processor until the mixture is well combined and vibrant green. Add a little more olive oil if the mixture is too dry.
- Season flathead with salt and pepper, then press one-quarter of the crumb mixture onto each fillet, making sure the crust evenly coats the fish; add more olive oil if necessary for crumbs to stick.
- Place crumbed flathead on top of fennel and tomatoes, then drizzle with olive oil, season with salt and bake for 12-15 minutes or until cooked through; the exact time depends on the thickness of the fillets.
- Divide fennel, tomatoes and fish between 4 plates, then squeeze with lemon juice and serve with a final drizzle of olive oil.

Beef in the Italian Style

1 × 450 g (2.5 cm thick) piece rump
(I use Coorong Angus beef tender-
stretched rump)

2 stalks rosemary, leaves picked
and chopped

extra virgin olive oil, for cooking

sea salt

¼ cup balsamic vinegar or vino cotto,
plus extra for drizzling

freshly ground black pepper

100 g Parmigiano Reggiano, shaved

generous bunch of rocket leaves, to serve

SERVES 4

I owe the idea for this recipe to Salvatore Pepe of Adelaide restaurant Cibo. Having first tasted this dish there, I took the principle of it, but instead of using a mouth-watering fillet of beef like Salvatore, which is the traditional cut for this dish, I've used a thick slice from the back cut of rump. Drizzling the meat with balsamic or vino cotto during the critical resting period certainly adds something very special – I recommend placing the meat to rest on a plate so that you don't lose any of the delicious resting juices. It is also absolutely crucial to carve the steak against the grain. This is a great way to serve a perfect piece of beef.

- Take beef out of the refrigerator 1 hour before you plan to cook it to bring it to room temperature.
- Rub beef with rosemary and olive oil, then season with salt. Cook on a very hot char-grill plate for about 2 minutes on each side, then turn on its edge to cook the fat for a couple of minutes; the idea is to sear it quickly over really high heat. Reduce heat to medium and cook for 3–4 minutes for medium-rare.
- Transfer to a serving plate, splash with balsamic or vino cotto and a little more olive oil and leave to rest for about 8 minutes (that is, double the cooking time). Season with salt and pepper, then carve against the grain into thick slices.
- Serve beef drizzled with a little more balsamic and olive oil, with shaved Parmigiano and rocket leaves to the side.

Slow-cooked Beef Fillet with Crushed Black Pepper and Balsamic

1 × 1–1.2 kg beef fillet (I use Coorong Angus beef), sinew trimmed

1 tablespoon crushed black peppercorns

2 teaspoons rosemary, roughly chopped

2 teaspoons thyme, roughly chopped

3 cloves garlic, thinly sliced

3–4 fresh bay leaves

¼ cup vino cotto or balsamic vinegar

sea salt

extra virgin olive oil, for cooking

SERVES 4–6

Recently my friend Sydney chef Kylie Kwong cooked a beef fillet in a domestic oven for dinner for a very special person in both of our lives. I couldn't believe how beautiful it was and thought it had to be the simplest way ever to prepare dinner for friends – just put it in the oven and walk away. In my recipe, I've introduced my mix of herbs and spices and seared the fillet just before serving so that has a lovely caramelised exterior, but you don't even need to do that. I also added the extra touch of vino cotto or balsamic.

- Tuck the skinny tail end of the beef under the fillet, then secure with kitchen string. Tie the rest of the fillet at 4 cm intervals and place in a roasting pan. Mix pepper, rosemary and thyme and rub all over beef, then top with garlic and bay leaves. Pour over balsamic, cover with plastic film and leave in the refrigerator to marinate for a couple of hours or overnight, turning occasionally.
- Remove fillet from refrigerator and leave for 1 hour to come to room temperature.
- Preheat fan-forced oven to 70°C (158°F).
- Remove beef from marinade and pat dry with paper towel, then place in a clean roasting pan, drizzle with olive oil and roast for 4 hours.
- If you wish to sear the beef to give it a caramelised appearance, when you remove the beef from the oven rub it with a little salt. Heat a splash of olive oil in a large frying pan over high heat, then add beef and seal on all sides quickly until coloured. Remove from pan and leave to rest for 20–30 minutes. The beef will be beautifully pink all the way through.
- Cut into thick slices and serve.

Warm Squid, Leek and Caper Salad

4 pencil leeks, trimmed and
cut into 12 cm lengths

extra virgin olive oil, for cooking

sea salt and freshly ground black pepper

2 tablespoons salted capers, rinsed

1 × 4 g packet squid ink

1 large lemon, zest removed with a
potato peeler in wide strips, then juiced

¼ cup verjuice

2 fresh bay leaves

2 tablespoons marjoram leaves

100 g unsalted butter, chopped

500 g squid tubes, cleaned and
cut into rings (or use cleaned baby
squid and cut in half lengthways)

plain flour, for dusting

½ cup flat-leaf parsley leaves

SERVES 4

You can tell that I like squid – I cook it in so many different ways and want to encourage others to do the same. It's not all that long ago that squid were only used for bait in Australia, with the exception of those with a Mediterranean or Asian background, who knew so well what the rest of us were missing. Whilst I cook the squid here in nut-brown butter, if it makes more sense to you, use extra virgin olive oil instead. The biggest tip I can give you is to only just cook the squid. However, if you've either cooked it a little too much or not quite enough, a generous squeeze of lemon juice will help to remedy both problems; it will either 'relax' the overcooked meat or 'cook' the underdone squid a little more.

- Brush leeks with olive oil and season with salt and pepper. Grill on a hot char-grill plate for about 5 minutes on each side or until caramelised and collapsed. Set aside.
- Shallow-fry capers in 2 teaspoons olive oil in a small frying pan over medium heat until crisp, then set aside.
- Squeeze squid ink into a bowl and add a little of the lemon juice, then set aside.
- Place lemon zest, verjuice and bay leaves in a saucepan and simmer over low heat for 5 minutes or until lemon zest is translucent. Remove from heat, then add marjoram, ¼ cup olive oil and remaining lemon juice to taste. Set aside.
- Melt butter in a frying pan over high heat until nut-brown (or use a splash of olive oil if you prefer). Toss the squid in a plastic bag with flour seasoned with salt, then shake squid to remove excess flour. Pan-fry squid in batches for about 1 minute on each side or until golden; each batch needs to sizzle a little the moment it hits the pan.
- Toss squid, leeks and parsley together and drizzle with squid ink mixture, then with verjuice mixture. Scatter salad with crisp capers and serve.

Pork Belly in Shiraz

1 × 850 g pork belly, skin scored in a diamond pattern

sea salt

2 tablespoons extra virgin olive oil

12 golden shallots, peeled

6 cloves garlic, peeled

200 ml shiraz

¼ cup aged red-wine vinegar

4 stalks rosemary

6 stalks thyme

2 fresh bay leaves

1 teaspoon fennel seeds

1 cup chicken stock

1 tablespoon vino cotto

SERVES 4-6

I came up with this dish for a special dinner for my friends Peter and Marg Lehmann, of Peter Lehmann Wines, to celebrate three vintages of Peter's 'Mentor' Cabernet Shiraz (1994, 1996 and 2002). It was quite a tricky number to do, given the different qualities of the three vintages at play.

The dinner was held at the Grand Hyatt Melbourne and the team there was fantastic to work with, not at all minding us bringing in so many Barossan ingredients, including the Berkshire pork belly from the Lienert's farm at Sheoak Log. They were also incredibly open to us serving the feast Barossa-style, with all the food laid out on large platters to be shared. (Not quite the norm in a five star hotel!)

I salt the pork the night before to increase its moistness and intensify the flavour.

- Rub pork generously with salt, then leave in the refrigerator overnight. Next day, rinse salt off, soak pork in a bowl of water for 10 minutes, then remove and pat dry with paper towels.
- Preheat fan-forced oven to 140°C (284°F).
- Heat olive oil in a heavy-based frying pan over high heat, then add pork and brown on all sides. Remove pork and set aside. Add shallots and garlic to pan and cook for 5 minutes or until browned.
- Combine wine, vinegar, rosemary, thyme, bay leaves, fennel seeds and stock in a cast-iron casserole, then bring to the boil over high heat. Add pork, skin side-down, shallots and garlic and reduce heat to low. Cover and cook in the oven for 90 minutes, then remove the lid and cook for another 1 hour. Remove pork, onions and garlic and keep warm.
- Boil braising liquid over high heat until reduced and syrupy, then add vino cotto.
- Just before serving, remove the bones from the pork and cut the meat into thick slices. This is so rich and luscious that I like to serve it with bitter leafy greens like wilted chicory and boiled waxy potatoes.

Chicken Braised with Figs, Honey and Vinegar

extra virgin olive oil, for cooking

2 red onions, roughly chopped

2 teaspoons chopped lemon thyme

2 teaspoons chopped rosemary

4 large ripe figs, halved

4 large Barossa or other corn-fed chicken marylands (thigh and drumstick joints), thighs and drumsticks separated

sea salt

1 stick cinnamon

½ cup chicken stock

½ cup verjuice

2 tablespoons sherry vinegar

zest of 1 lemon, removed in wide strips with a potato peeler

2 tablespoons honey

chopped flat-leaf parsley (optional), to serve

GRILLED SEMOLINA (OPTIONAL)

2 cups milk

2 cups water

1 fresh bay leaf

1 cup instant semolina

1 teaspoon salt

plain flour, for dusting

extra virgin olive oil, for cooking

unsalted butter, for cooking

SERVES 4

Here is another of those one-pot dishes that your family and friends will love. The trick is to use a shallow baking dish so that the ingredients come almost to the top of the dish; that way, when you drizzle the chicken skin with honey it will caramelise beautifully as so much more of it is exposed to the heat than if cooked in a deeper dish. If figs aren't available, then add par-cooked and peeled baby onions tossed with vinegar, raisins and rosemary instead, to keep in tune with the lovely sweet-sour flavours of the dish.

I like to serve this with grilled semolina, however, the semolina needs to be cooked at least 2–3 hours in advance (or the day before) and chilled in the refrigerator until firm before char-grilling. If you don't have the time for this, then serve the chicken with boiled waxy potatoes or some creamy soft polenta (see recipe page 103) instead.

- If you plan to serve this with grilled semolina, then bring milk, water and bay leaf to the boil over high heat in a saucepan, then remove from the heat and leave to infuse for 20 minutes. Strain into a heavy-based saucepan, discarding bay leaf, then bring to the boil again. Reduce heat to low. Slowly pour in semolina and add salt, then whisk continuously to combine for 4–5 minutes, ensuring there are no lumpy bits. Grease a baking dish with olive oil, then pour semolina mixture into the dish. Cover with plastic film and leave to set in the refrigerator for at least 2–3 hours.

- Preheat fan-forced oven to 200°C (400°F).

- Heat a splash of olive oil in a frying pan over medium heat, then add onions, thyme and rosemary and sauté for 5 minutes or until softened. Transfer to a shallow flameproof baking dish. Quickly sauté fig halves in the frying pan and transfer to onion mixture in baking dish.

- Sprinkle chicken pieces with salt and place on top of onions and figs, then add cinnamon, stock, verjuice, vinegar and lemon zest. Drizzle with honey, then bake for 30–35 minutes or until chicken is cooked, basting occasionally with pan juices. Remove from oven and transfer chicken and figs to a dish to rest; keep warm. Simmer pan juices over high heat until reduced and syrupy.

- If you've prepared the semolina, then cut it on the diagonal into 7 cm pieces. Lightly dust each piece with flour, then heat a splash of olive oil and a knob of butter in a char-grill pan over high heat and cook semolina pieces for 2 minutes on each side or until warmed through and grill marks appear.

- Return chicken and figs to sauce, then drizzle with olive oil and scatter with parsley, if using. Serve at once with grilled semolina, if desired.

Pot-roasted Rabbit with Prunes and Mustard

1 × 1.6 kg farmed rabbit, with liver
and kidneys intact

2 stalks sage

6 stalks lemon thyme

2 tablespoons Dijon mustard

¼ cup extra virgin olive oil,
plus extra for cooking

12 small pickling onions

60 g unsalted butter

100 g pitted prunes

⅓ cup verjuice, plus extra for cooking

½ cup chicken stock

sea salt and freshly ground black pepper

SERVES 4

I love to eat rabbit, and have cooked it ever since I came to live in South Australia. Whilst wild rabbit is one of the hardest ingredients to cook successfully (more often than not being spoilt by overcooking), farmed rabbit is another matter altogether. It is plump, with a layer of fat that makes it so much easier to keep moist during cooking – it can even be barbecued, although not over a fierce heat (something I'd never even contemplate doing with wild rabbit). You could also try barbecuing the marinated rabbit here, saving the prunes and cooked baby onions for a post-cooking 'bath' with verjuice and extra virgin olive oil – just an idea!

- Joint rabbit into front and back legs and saddle, then cut the saddle into 3 pieces. Using a flexible filleting knife, remove sinew from the saddle, then remove and reserve liver and kidneys. Alternatively, ask your butcher to do this.

- Combine rabbit pieces with sage, thyme, mustard and olive oil. Cover with plastic film and leave to marinate at room temperature for 1 hour.

- Meanwhile, blanch onions in a saucepan of simmering water for 10 minutes. Cool slightly, then peel and set aside.

- Heat 40 g butter with a little olive oil added in a heavy-based frying pan over medium heat until nut-brown. Add rabbit pieces and gently cook over low heat, turning occasionally, for 4 minutes or until lightly coloured, then remove and set aside. Add a little more olive oil if necessary, then add onions and cook for 5 minutes or until golden. Return rabbit pieces to pan, add prunes, then deglaze pan with verjuice.

- Add chicken stock and simmer, covered, over medium heat for 6 minutes. Turn rabbit pieces over, then reduce temperature to low and cook until tender. The saddle pieces are cooked when they feel pliable to the touch and each muscle separates easily from the leg. If cooked, then remove and set aside to rest. Otherwise continue cooking until leg pieces are tender, taking care not to overcook. Remove rabbit from pan, then simmer pan juices over high heat until reduced and syrupy.

- Heat a small frying pan over high heat, then melt remaining butter until nut-brown. Add liver and kidneys and cook for 1 minute or so on each side, then deglaze pan with a splash of verjuice, if desired.

- Return rabbit pieces to sauce, along with liver and kidneys, then season to taste with salt and pepper and serve. I like to serve this with lots of soft polenta (see recipe on page 103).

Potato Gnocchi with Prawns

750 g nicola or other waxy
potatoes, scrubbed

2 free-range eggs, lightly beaten

2½ teaspoons salt

125 g plain flour

170 g cold unsalted butter,
chopped into small pieces

⅓ cup verjuice

40 sage leaves (about 1 bunch)

extra virgin olive oil, for cooking

12 raw king prawns or yabbies,
peeled and cleaned, with tails intact

sea salt and freshly ground black pepper

SERVES 4

I love to make gnocchi, and over the years have done so in many different ways, finally reaching the point where I wanted to write a definitive recipe, not only for myself but for my family as well, as it is such a firm favourite.

I'd made my gnocchi with potato, flour and butter for years, but after eating Alex Herbert's version at her Sydney restaurant Bird Cow Fish, made with potato, flour and egg and served with burnt butter and prawns, I wanted to take another look at my method. Of course, not doing anything by halves, I decided to do a blind trial of both types of dough. Not content with that, I then divided the two doughs, kneading one half of each and just pulling the other half together. The results were fascinating – the kneaded butter-based gnocchi were lighter than the egg gnocchi, while the unkneaded butter one fell apart when poached. The kneaded egg-based gnocchi were a little tough, so for me, the winner was the unkneaded egg-based gnocchi, which is the way that Alex makes it. When I think about how much I respect Alex's cooking, I could have just gone with her method; however, proving it for myself was immensely satisfying.

The idea of putting prawns with gnocchi comes from Alex, but my take is to do it with yabbies instead when I can get them – either way, it is a beautiful dish.

♦ Steam unpeeled potatoes for 30 minutes or until cooked through but not falling apart. Set aside until just cool enough to handle, then peel. Press hot potatoes through a mouli or potato ricer into a bowl, then add eggs and salt. Place flour in a rectangular shape on the bench. Spread potatoes over the flour, then quickly mix with a pastry scraper until it comes together to form a dough. Divide dough into quarters, then shape each quarter into a long 2.5 cm wide sausage. Cut off 1.5 cm pieces, then gently press the tops with the back of a fork's tines to leave an indentation, which will help the gnocchi to pick up more sauce.

♦ Preheat fan-forced oven to 200°C (400°F).

♦ Bring salted water to the boil in a large deep frying pan and cook gnocchi in batches until they float to the surface (if just made, this could take as little as 30 seconds). Drain well and transfer to a flat dish.

♦ Place 150 g of the butter and sage leaves in a large flat baking dish (mine is 32 × 28 × 3 cm), spreading butter and sage evenly. Bake for 5 minutes or until sage begins to cook.

♦ Increase oven temperature to 230°C (475°F). Transfer poached gnocchi to baking dish with butter and sage, then bake for 5 minutes. Toss the dish to flip the gnocchi or turn each one over with a pair of tongs, then drizzle with ¼ cup of the verjuice and return to the oven for another 3 minutes.

♦ Meanwhile, heat remaining butter and a splash of olive oil in a frying pan over high heat until nut-brown, then reduce heat to medium and gently sauté prawns or yabbies, if using, until pink and just cooked through. Season to taste with salt and pepper and deglaze with remaining verjuice. Transfer prawns or yabbies and pan juices to gnocchi and gently combine.

♦ Divide gnocchi and prawns or yabbies between 4 bowls, then serve immediately.

Veal Cutlets with Garlic

2 heads garlic, tops cut off
and discarded

1 teaspoon extra virgin olive oil,
plus extra for drizzling

2 tablespoons mascarpone

2-3 slices day-old white bread,
crusts removed

1 teaspoon chopped thyme

1 tablespoon chopped flat-leaf parsley

1 teaspoon finely grated lemon zest

sea salt and freshly ground black pepper

4 thick double-cut veal cutlets

plain flour, for dusting

1-2 free-range eggs, beaten

40 g unsalted butter

lemon wedges, to serve

SERVES 4

I remember the sweet, moist crumbed veal chops of my childhood – in those days they were a special treat. The roasted heads of garlic, so nutty and sweet, can easily be prepared in advance and just warmed again while you pan-fry the veal. No sauce is needed here – just a good squeeze of lemon juice before serving. It is important to buy double cutlets as not only are they luscious but their thickness offers a better ratio of meat to breadcrumb coating.

- Preheat fan-forced oven to 180°C (350°F).
- Drizzle garlic with olive oil, then wrap in foil and roast for 40 minutes. Open up foil, then top with mascarpone and return to the oven for another 10 minutes.
- Meanwhile, process bread in a food processor until breadcrumbs form. Add herbs and lemon zest, then season with salt and pepper and process to combine.
- Just before returning garlic to the oven with the mascarpone, heat a large frying pan over medium-high heat. Toss cutlets in flour seasoned with salt and pepper, shaking to remove excess, then dip each cutlet into beaten egg, then into breadcrumb mixture. Heat butter and olive oil in the hot pan until butter turns nut-brown, then add cutlets. Cook cutlets on both sides until golden, then reduce heat to low to prevent crumbs from burning and cook for another 10-12 minutes.
- Serve veal cutlets with a squeeze of lemon juice and roasted garlic with mascarpone to the side.

Kibbeh

500 g lamb loin or leg fillet, sinew removed (or ask your butcher to mince it twice using the finest setting)

100 g finely cracked wheat (burghul)

1 teaspoon ground cumin

1 teaspoon ground allspice

1 teaspoon ground coriander

pinch of cayenne

sea salt

cos leaves or flatbread, to serve

TOPPING

extra virgin olive oil, for drizzling

pinch of sweet smoked paprika

1 golden shallot, very thinly sliced

1 spring onion, thinly sliced

finely grated zest and juice of 1 lemon

2 tablespoons chopped flat-leaf parsley

2 tablespoons chopped mint

sea salt and freshly ground black pepper

SERVES 4-6

My daughter Saskia introduced me to this dish. At the time she was producing milk-fed lamb, and had so much high-quality meat at her disposal (plus children who love raw meat) that it quickly became a family favourite.

It's a great dish for a hot summer's day; be sure to squeeze with lemon juice just before serving.

- If you are mincing our own meat, then make sure that it is super-cold before you start. Chop the cold meat into small pieces, then pulse briefly in a food processor, taking care not to purée. Place meat in a blender with remaining ingredients, then blend to a smooth paste; it should be fine but not over-processed. Press lamb mixture onto a plate.
- For the topping, drizzle lamb with olive oil. Sprinkle with paprika, shallot, spring onion, lemon zest and herbs. About 5-10 minutes before serving, squeeze over lemon juice, then season to taste with salt, if necessary, and pepper.
- Serve kibbeh with cos leaves or flatbread for scooping it up.

Glazed Leg of Ham

7 kg leg of ham, traditionally smoked

175 g soft-brown sugar

100 ml port

150 g dried figs (soak in warm water until plump) or Preserved Figs (see recipe page 52), halved widthways

150 g pitted prunes

150 g dried apricots

SERVES 16

What is Christmas without a good leg of ham on the table? For me it's a Berkshire (or another heritage breed) ham that my daughter Saskia brings to the table from the Lienert's farm, that she has had traditionally smoked. Using a heritage breed ham such as this will give you an amazingly superior result – and a ham without fat is a ham without flavour!

Given that food safety requirements specify that a minimum internal temperature needs to have been reached when the ham is produced, preferably speak to your supplier and let them know that you plan to glaze and cook the ham again so they can choose a 'just-cooked' ham rather than a 'well-cooked' one. Whilst the glaze on its own is pretty terrific, you can either use two 360 gram jars of Maggie Beer Pickled Figs, drained and halved widthways, for topping the ham or the dried figs, prunes and apricots specified here to make a ham that deserves being served as the centrepiece of your Christmas table.

- Preheat fan-forced oven to 250°C (525°F) or as high as you can.
- Cut away the leathery skin from the top of the ham, taking care not to remove any fat from under the skin; you are after a 5 mm–1 cm layer of fat.
- Mix sugar and port into a paste and brush it over the top and sides of the ham several times. Score fat quite deeply into a diamond pattern, taking care not to cut through to the meat – the diamonds should be about the size of the dried fruit you are using to decorate the ham. Brush with glaze until you have used about half of it.
- Place ham in a roasting pan and bake, brushing with the glaze occasionally, for 15 minutes or until the fat starts to caramelise. Watch that the base of the pan doesn't start to burn; add a little water to the pan if necessary as soon as the glaze starts to caramelise.
- Carefully attach dried or preserved fruit to the middle of the diamonds with toothpicks, arranging them in alternating rows of each fruit (or use drained and halved Maggie Beer Pickled Figs as I've done here – see opposite). Brush the remaining glaze over the ham, taking care not to dislodge the glaze or fruit. Bake the ham for another 15-20 minutes or until it is beautifully glazed, then leave to cool before carving and serving.

Porterhouse of Suffolk Lamb with Caramelised Radicchio

1 × 1.1 kg Suffolk lamb porterhouse

½ cup extra virgin olive oil

5 cloves garlic, roughly chopped

2 tablespoons roughly chopped rosemary

sea salt and freshly ground black pepper

CARAMELISED RADICCHIO

80 g unsalted butter, chopped

extra virgin olive oil, for cooking

1 small head radicchio, outer leaves discarded and cut lengthways into eighths (about 200 g)

⅓ cup vino cotto

sea salt and freshly ground black pepper

finely chopped chives or flat-leaf parsley (optional), to serve

SERVES 6

I'm a great fan of Richard Gunner of Feast! Fine Foods' Coorong Angus beef. I've seldom met a more enthusiastic and knowledgeable producer. Richard has now added another string to his bow: his delectable Suffolk lamb. The flavour and texture of this lamb is truly exceptional. Whilst Richard's lamb may not be readily accessible in other states, it provides inspiration for searching out local specialist lamb producers, as the better the breed, growing conditions and care, the better the flavour by a huge margin. Richard is not only a producer but a meat specialist too. He has four butcher shops for selling his own produce directly to the public, so he is constantly experimenting with new (and old) cuts and the best ways to cook them. His idea for cooking lamb porterhouse is a great one: the fat is first rendered on a hot grill-plate, then the lamb is roasted using a low temperature to ensure succulence; finally, the individual slices are caramelised again on the hot grill-plate, making for a stunning end result.

- Score lamb fat in a diamond pattern, then marinate lamb with olive oil, garlic and rosemary for at least 1 hour, turning occasionally.

- Preheat fan-forced oven to 160°C (325°F).

- Heat a char-grill pan or barbecue grill-plate until smoking hot, then season lamb generously with salt and pepper and brown on all sides, including the fat.

- Transfer lamb to a roasting pan and roast for 20 minutes for beautifully pink, yet cooked lamb; if you have a meat thermometer the internal temperature should be 55°C (131°F). Remove from oven and leave to rest in a warm place.

- Meanwhile, for caramelised radicchio, heat butter and a splash of olive oil in a frying pan over high heat until butter is foamy. Add radicchio and sauté for 3 minutes or until it collapses and is golden and caramelised on both sides. Deglaze pan with vino cotto and cook until it is reduced and syrupy, then season with salt and pepper and scatter with chives or parsley, if using.

- Evenly cut lamb into 8 thick slices, then grill in a hot char-grill pan or a hot barbecue grill plate for a few minutes on both sides.

- Serve lamb with caramelised radicchio.

Confit of Rabbit with Pancetta, Pine Nuts and Raisins

1 × 1.6 kg rabbit

2 tablespoons finely chopped rosemary, plus 2 tablespoons rosemary leaves

4 cloves garlic, peeled

1 tablespoon thyme leaves

½ teaspoon sea salt

3 fresh bay leaves

2-3 cups extra virgin olive oil, for cooking

⅓ cup pine nuts

⅓ cup raisins

verjuice, for soaking

8 thin slices round pancetta, thinly sliced

1½ cups roughly torn ciabatta

1 tablespoon rinsed and finely chopped preserved lemon rind

⅔ cup flat-leaf parsley leaves

lemon wedges, to serve

SERVES 4

I've always thought that the ability to cook rabbit well is the mark of a good cook. So many people overcook rabbit, particularly in the days when only wild rabbit were available and the tradition was to cook it and cook it, then cook it some more. My first epiphany with rabbit was back in the 1980s when my friend Stephanie Alexander invited me to be a 'fly on the wall' in the kitchen of her wonderful Stephanie's restaurant, to see firsthand how it worked. It was so cutting edge and incredibly frenetic – full houses every night – with one or two flamboyant French chefs as well as Stephanie behind the burners. This was the first time I'd ever seen rabbit being cooked in joints, the reason being that the saddle, front legs and back legs all take different amounts of time to cook, not to mention the liver and kidneys which cook in a matter of minutes. This is the way I've cooked rabbit ever since.

Now that farmed rabbit is readily available it is much easier to cook because it's had a short, well-fed life. Larger producers offer legs and saddles separately, although, being such a relatively small and new industry, not all producers will sell rabbits jointed.

Making confit involves immersing an ingredient such as rabbit or duck in its own fat or oil. The key to success here is cooking the rabbit so slowly and over such a low temperature that the surface of the confit ingredients barely break a simmer during the cooking process.

- Remove front and back legs from rabbit, then cut saddle into 3 even pieces, keeping the flaps intact. Set aside liver and kidneys. Rub chopped rosemary into rabbit pieces, then cover with plastic film and refrigerate for 2 hours in summer or the tropics or at room temperature during cooler times of the year.

- Preheat fan-forced oven to 110°C (230°F).

- Toss rabbit pieces with garlic, rosemary leaves, thyme, salt and bay leaves, adding a splash of olive oil to moisten. Place larger hind legs, garlic and herbs in an oven-proof casserole just large enough to fit rabbit pieces snugly in 1 layer, then add front legs and saddle pieces, with flaps wrapped around them to keep them moist during cooking. Cover rabbit completely with warm olive oil (warmed in the microwave using the 'defrost' setting for 5 minutes).

- Cook rabbit, uncovered, in the oven for 90 minutes or until rabbit pieces are tender. The saddle pieces will cook before the legs, so check them after 45 minutes or so; if the meat is white, cooked through and tender to the touch, remove and set aside. Continue cooking legs for another 45 minutes or until they are cooked through and tender to the touch. Return all rabbit to the oil and leave to cool.

- Drain off most of the oil, leaving just enough to keep rabbit, herbs and garlic moist. Remove rabbit meat from bones, discarding bones, skin and gristle, then set aside; you should have about 2½ cups meat.

- Preheat fan-forced oven to 180°C (350°F).

- Place pine nuts on a baking tray and roast for 5-8 minutes or until golden. Leave to cool.

- Soak raisins in enough verjuice to cover until plump and hydrated. Drain, reserving 1 tablespoon of the verjuice.

- Cook pancetta in a dry frying pan over medium heat until crisp, then set aside to drain on paper towel.

- Heat ¼ cup olive oil in a frying pan over high heat, then add torn ciabatta and cook until crisp and golden. Drain on paper towels. Add rabbit pieces, garlic and herbs to pan with a little of the rabbit juices and reserved verjuice. Add pine nuts, raisins, pancetta and preserved lemon. Toss all the ingredients together vigorously, then remove from heat.

- Add parsley to rabbit mixture, then serve with lemon wedges to the side.

Pot-roasted Pheasant
with Apples and Calvados

40 g unsalted butter, plus extra
for cooking

extra virgin olive oil, for cooking

2 granny smith apples, peeled,
cored and cut into 8 wedges

zest of 1 lemon, removed in wide strips
with a potato peeler, plus juice of lemon

3 stalks lemon thyme, leaves picked

2 fresh bay leaves

2 × 900 g pheasants

sea salt

¼ cup Calvados or apple brandy
(Scotch whisky also works well)

2 tablespoons verjuice

1 cup chicken stock

⅓ cup pouring cream

freshly ground black pepper

1 × 2 cm piece ginger, finely grated

chopped chives, to serve

SERVES 6-8

I've cooked pheasant in so many ways than I could possibly remember, given that I served it every day of the nearly fifteen years that we ran the Pheasant Farm restaurant. The first pheasant recipe I ever cooked was in the 70s and it came from Elizabeth David's groundbreaking cookbook, *French Provincial Cooking*. These days I cook a lot less pheasant, but here I've gone back to the bones, so to speak, of Elizabeth David's recipe. However, this is a much lighter dish than the original, and it contains one or two surprises – namely the addition of ginger and lemon thyme. I also heard there was an Australian producer making apple brandy and wanted to give it a try.

If your guests haven't eaten pheasant before, you may need to warn them that the drumsticks contain very sharp sinews that can be dangerous to eat if you aren't aware of them. You can extract them with a pair of pliers before serving by cutting around the base of the drumsticks to expose the sinews, then pull them out – or let your guests know to only chew on the meatier ends.

- Preheat fan-forced oven to 180°C (350°F).
- Heat butter with a splash of olive oil in a cast-iron casserole over medium heat, then add apples, lemon zest, thyme and bay leaves and sauté for 3 minutes or until apples are coloured. Remove and set aside.
- Season pheasants with salt, then add a little more butter and oil to the pan, if necessary, and gently brown the pheasant until golden on all sides. Place pheasants on their sides. Deglaze pan with Calvados or apple brandy and verjuice, then add chicken stock and bring to the simmer over medium heat. Return apples, herbs and lemon zest to the pan.
- Cover with a tight-fitting lid and roast for 10 minutes. Turn pheasants over and cook for another 10 minutes. To check if birds are cooked, pull a leg gently away from each breast and check that there is no sign of pinkness; if there is, then cook until no signs of pinkness remain. Remove pheasants from the pan and leave to rest in a warm place, breast side-down, for 10-15 minutes. Either cut pheasants into quarters or remove legs and carve the breasts.
- Meanwhile, bring pan juices to the boil over high heat, then remove from heat and add cream, pepper and ginger. Pour sauce over pheasant, then scatter with chopped chives and serve immediately.

Beef Tagine with Dried Fruit

1.5 kg oyster blade steak, cut into 4-5 cm pieces

1 tablespoon ras el hanout (Moroccan spice blend available from specialty food stores)

¼ cup blanched almonds (optional)

extra virgin olive oil, for cooking

1 large onion, roughly chopped

2 cloves garlic, chopped

4 saffron threads

sea salt and freshly ground black pepper

1 large stick cinnamon

4 beef marrow bones or 4 osso bucco

24 dried apricots

18 large prunes, pitted

2 teaspoons rosewater

¼ cup soft-brown sugar

chopped flat-leaf parsley and couscous or freekeh (see recipe page 20), to serve

SERVES 6-8

This is another recipe inspired by our recent holiday in Morocco. I found the best food to be had was prepared by the women who worked in *riads*, the very small hotels of no more than eight or so rooms. During our stay in Essaouira, we enjoyed an exceptional beef tagine and were fortunate enough to be allowed to watch and take notes as the ladies worked in the kitchen to prepare this magnificent dish.

Whilst tagines are cooked every day (and everywhere) in Morocco, for me the robust flavours make this is very much a winter dish. Although this tagine can be served immediately, its flavour improves if made a day or two in advance. This also allows you to remove any excess fat that may solidify on the surface as it chills in the refrigerator.

- Mix beef and ras el hanout together, cover with plastic film and leave to marinate at room temperature for about 1 hour.
- Preheat fan-forced oven to 180°C (350°F).
- Place almonds, if using, on a baking tray and roast for 8-10 minutes or until golden, then leave to cool.
- Reduce oven temperature to 150°C (300°F).
- Heat a splash of olive oil in a heavy-based frying pan over low-medium heat and sauté onion and garlic for 6-8 minutes or until translucent. Add saffron, then transfer to a bowl and set aside.
- Heat a little more olive oil in the same pan, then brown the meat in batches, seasoning with salt and pepper as you go.
- Place beef, onion mixture, cinnamon and marrow bones in a large cast-iron casserole with a tight-fitting lid (my Le Creuset one is perfect for this) and add ¼ cup water. Cook, covered with a tight-fitting lid, in the oven for about 1 hour or until meat is just tender.
- Meanwhile, put apricots, prunes, rosewater and brown sugar into a small saucepan and add just enough water to cover the fruit. Bring to the boil, then reduce heat to low and simmer for 10 minutes or until fruit plumps up. The fruit will absorb almost all of the liquid.
- After the meat has cooked for 1 hour, add dried fruit mixture and stir to combine. Continue to cook for another 45-60 minutes or until the meat is tender, but not falling apart (this could take up to another hour longer, depending on oven, cooking vessel and quality of meat used). You may find there is a lot of liquid left over - if so, remove meat and fruit from the pan and reduce liquid over high heat until a little syrupy. Return meat and fruit to the pan and season to taste, if necessary.
- Spoon the meat and fruit into serving bowls or plates, then scatter with roasted almonds, if using, and a little chopped parsley. Top each serve with some of the cooked marrow spooned out of the bones. Serve with cous cous to the side.

Spicy Pork and Apple Pasties

⅓ cup pine nuts

½ cup verjuice

¼ cup dried currants

⅓ cup dried apples, chopped

extra virgin olive oil, for cooking

1 small onion, finely chopped

2 cloves garlic, finely chopped

1 tablespoon ground ginger

1 tablespoon ground cinnamon

2 tablespoons honey

500 g minced pork

¼ preserved lemon, flesh removed and rind rinsed and finely chopped

2 free-range eggs, lightly beaten

¼ cup flat-leaf parsley, chopped

1½ teaspoons sea salt

freshly ground black pepper

1 free-range egg, beaten with 1 tablespoon pouring cream

GLUTEN-FREE PASTRY

500 g chilled cream cheese, cut into chunks

300 g chilled unsalted butter, chopped

4 cups gluten-free flour (see page 174), plus extra for dusting

2 tablespoons salt

8 g xanthum gum (available from health food stores and large supermarkets)

MAKES 8

I had great fun putting together my take on the pasty, a South Australian favourite. When filming for my television show, we went to Burra, a delightful town in mid-northern South Australia with a history of copper mining. In the process of immersing myself in background research, I decided it would be fun to take a different slant on the traditional concept of a pasty, one version of which contained meat at one end and apple, for dessert, at the other. I incorporated the apple with the meat, then added currants and pine nuts for a Sicilian touch, creating pasties that are full of flavour.

If you have any pastry scraps leftover at the end, pull them together to form a flat rectangle, wrap it in plastic film and store it in the refrigerator, where it will keep for a few weeks. It can be used to make a quick cheese tart or topped with fruit such as apples, pears or berries for a sweet tart.

- Preheat fan-forced oven to 180° (350°F).

- Place pine nuts on a baking tray and roast for about 5-8 minutes or until golden. Remove and leave to cool.

- Place ¼ cup of the verjuice in each of 2 small saucepans, then add the currants to one and the dried apples to the other. Heat both pans gently over low heat for a few minutes, then set aside to plump and cool.

- Heat a splash of olive oil in a small frying pan over low-medium heat, then sauté onion and garlic for 10 minutes or until translucent but not coloured. Add ginger and cinnamon and cook for another minute or so, until the spices give off a rich scent; take care not to burn them. Remove from heat, stir in honey and leave to cool.

- Put minced pork, pine nuts, cooled onion mixture, soaked currants and apple mixtures (including the soaking juices), preserved lemon, eggs, parsley, salt and pepper in a large bowl and mix thoroughly. Cover and refrigerate until ready to use.

- For the gluten-free pastry, pulse cream cheese and butter in a food processor until combined. Add flour, salt and xanthum gum, then whiz to just combine, scraping down the side of the bowl with a spatula. If the pastry doesn't come together to form a ball after a few pulses, add a little chilled water (1 table-spoon at the most).

- Turn dough out onto a bench dusted with a little extra gluten-free flour. Bring dough together with your hands, then knead for 3-4 minutes or until it comes together to form a ball. Although this pastry does not need to be chilled for a long time, it is easier to handle if placed in the refrigerator for 5 minutes before rolling out.

- Divide dough into 8 even pieces, then roll out each piece, one at a time, between 2 pieces of greased baking paper to make a 3 mm thick round.

- Divide filling into eighths, then place one-eight on the bottom half of each pastry round. Fold pastry over to encase the filling, then fold over the edges thickly to seal, trimming off any excess pastry. Brush with egg wash made by beating egg with cream, then place on a baking tray lined with baking paper and refrigerate for 10-15 minutes.

- Preheat fan-forced oven to 230°C (475°F).

- Bake pasties for 20-25 minutes or until golden, then serve.

Steak Sandwiches with Skirt Steak

1 × 600 g piece skirt steak,
fat trimmed, cut into 4 thin slices

¼ cup extra virgin olive oil

1 stalk rosemary, leaves picked
and chopped

8 thick slices ciabatta or other
rustic wood-fired bread

2 cloves garlic, halved

1 × 225 g tin sliced beetroot, drained

sea salt and freshly ground black pepper

rocket leaves, to serve

ROCKET MAYONNAISE

4 large free-range egg yolks,
at room temperature

pinch of sea salt

2 teaspoons Dijon mustard (optional)

1½ cups rocket leaves, finely chopped

2 tablespoons lemon juice

1 cup extra virgin olive oil

1 cup vegetable or grape seed oil

freshly ground black pepper

boiling water (optional), to thin

CARAMELISED ONIONS

40 g unsalted butter

4 large red onions, thinly sliced

¼ cup soft-brown sugar

¼ cup red-wine vinegar

SERVES 4

Skirt steak is mostly ignored. But in commercial kitchens it's often the cut that chefs will cook as a titbit for themselves – I wonder whether this is because the public wouldn't recognise it on a menu? However, it is revered by the cuisines of other cultures, including that of the French, and is inexpensive to boot. It is a great cut for cooking very quickly and serving rare, so don't just limit it to making steak sandwiches. If you manage to buy skirt steak in one whole piece it is a very odd shape. Because it is thicker at one end you either need to divide it into two portions so it cooks evenly or butterfly the thicker side out to make a piece of even thickness all the way along.

- Marinate steaks in olive oil and rosemary for several hours.
- For the rocket mayonnaise, blend egg yolks, salt and mustard, if using, in a food processor, then add rocket and continue blending. With the motor running, add about 1½ tablespoons of the lemon juice, blending until smooth, then begin adding the combined oils slowly, a drop at a time to start with. Once the mixture starts to thicken, add remaining oil in a slow, steady stream. When all the oil has been added, taste, then season with pepper and add remaining lemon juice, if desired. For a steak sandwich, the mayonnaise should be thick, but add a little boiling water if you prefer it a little thinner. Cover closely with plastic film and refrigerate until required.
- For the caramelised onions, melt butter in a frying pan over medium heat, then add onions and cook for 5 minutes. Add sugar, then continue cooking for another 10 minutes, stirring frequency to prevent burning. Reduce heat to low and cook for another 15 minutes, stirring occasionally. Deglaze pan with vinegar and cook for 5 minutes or until reduced and syrupy. Set aside.
- Heat a char-grill pan as hot as possible. Sear steaks on one side for 1½–2 minutes, then turn and cook for another 1 minute or until cooked to your liking. Remove and leave to rest in a warm place.
- Grill sliced bread in a clean, hot, dry char-grill pan until grill marks appear, then rub with cut garlic. Top 4 slices of toasted bread with some of the onion mixture, a dollop of rocket mayonnaise, a piece of steak, some beetroot slices and some rocket leaves (or serve these to the side), then season to taste with salt and pepper. Spread a little of the mayonnaise over the remaining pieces of toast and place on top to complete the sandwiches.
- Serve steak sandwiches immediately, with extra mayonnaise to the side, if desired.

Steak and Oyster Pies

extra virgin olive oil, for cooking

1.5 kg oyster blade steak, cut into 1.5 cm pieces

sea salt and freshly ground black pepper

80 g unsalted butter, chopped

1 large onion, roughly chopped

1 large carrot, roughly chopped

1 stick celery, roughly chopped

250 g oyster mushrooms, chopped

1 teaspoon thyme, finely chopped

2 small fresh bay leaves

60 g plain flour

2 cups beef stock (as required)

1 cup stout (I use Guinness)

2 tablespoons kecap manis (thick soy sauce)

16 oysters, freshly shucked

LARD PASTRY

200 g plain flour

200 g self-raising flour

1 teaspoon salt

200 g lard, chopped

¾ cup cold water

1 free-range egg, beaten with 1 teaspoon pouring cream

MAKES 8

I love cooking so-called 'lesser' cuts of beef slowly over low-heat for a long period of time so that the connective tissues become gelatinous without overcooking the meat. Cuts such as the oyster blade I've used here, plus shin and beef cheeks, should be revered as they offer so much flavour, but you do need to have time on your side. Here I've cooked the meat for two hours, but it could be cooked all day in a crockpot set on low heat if you have one.

- Preheat fan-forced oven to 180°C (350°F).

- Heat a little olive oil in a large heavy-based frying pan over high heat. Season beef with salt and pepper, then, working in batches, add meat to the pan and brown on all sides.

- In a cast-iron casserole, heat butter and a splash of olive oil over medium heat, then add onion, carrot, celery and mushrooms and cook for 8–10 minutes or until just starting to caramelise. Add herbs and beef to the pan, then add flour and stir for a few minutes until flour is well distributed. Add 1 cup of the stock and the stout and kecap manis and stir to combine.

- Cover with a lid and cook in the oven for 2 hours or until meat is tender. Add more stock if you feel the meat needs to be moistened further, or add when the beef is cooking if the beef becomes too dry. Leave beef mixture to cool completely – overnight in the refrigerator is best.

- For the lard pastry, combine flours and salt in a large bowl, then rub in lard with your fingertips until the mixture resembles fine breadcrumbs. Slowly add enough water to bring the dough together, then knead for 3 minutes and form into a ball; don't be tempted to make this in a food processor as it will crumble on baking. Wrap in plastic film and chill in the refrigerator for 20 minutes.

- Preheat fan-forced oven to 220°C (450°F).

- Roll out pastry on a lightly floured bench, then use just under half of the pastry to line 8 small pie tins. Half-fill pastry cases with cold beef mixture, then top each with 2 freshly shucked oysters. Cut 8 rounds slightly bigger than the pie tins from remaining pastry and use to cover the meat and oysters. Do not re-roll pastry scraps to make the tops. Press down on edges to seal, then cut a slit in the middle of the pastry tops to let steam escape. Brush pastry with beaten egg and cream mixture.

- Bake pies for 15 minutes, then turn oven temperature down to 200°C (400°F) and cook for another 10 minutes or until pastry tops are golden.

- Serve pies at once.

Kangaroo Fillet with Beetroot and Anchovy Butter

2 × 400 g double (extra thick) kangaroo fillets

3 fresh bay leaves

1½ tablespoons juniper berries, crushed

4 wide strips orange zest, removed with a potato peeler, then cut into julienne

3–4 stalks thyme

1 clove garlic, thinly sliced

extra virgin olive oil, for drizzling

sea salt and freshly ground black pepper

4 medium-sized beetroot, leaves trimmed leaving 2 cm stalks attached

2 large handfuls rocket leaves

vino cotto, for drizzling

ANCHOVY BUTTER

1 × 45 g tin anchovies, drained and chopped

250 g unsalted butter, chopped and softened

1 tablespoon lemon juice

freshly ground black pepper

SERVES 4

I've been cooking kangaroo since the early 1980s, when selling it was first legalised in South Australia. Cheong Liew, then of Neddy's Restaurant, was the first to put kangaroo on restaurant tables and I followed his lead soon after. In the old days of the Pheasant Farm restaurant it was incredibly popular and certainly the second-most popular choice on the menu (the first – surprise, surprise – was pheasant!).

I love the flavour of roo, especially when I can order my favourite cut, the double-fillet, which has an amazing texture. Beetroot just works brilliantly with kangaroo, as does anchovy butter, so here I've combined the three to make one fantastic dish. Cooking the kangaroo on the barbecue is not only the simplest way, it also offers the best flavour; the only things to remember are to cook it rare and let it rest (a little longer than the cooking time is ideal). If you like your meat to be well done, then you could get away with serving it medium-rare if you must, otherwise forget this dish – you may as well eat boot leather.

- Marinate kangaroo with bay leaves, juniper, orange zest, thyme, garlic and a splash of olive oil for 2 hours in the refrigerator. Remove from the refrigerator for 1 hour before cooking and leave to come to room temperature.

- For the anchovy butter, mix chopped anchovies and butter, then stir in lemon juice and season to taste with pepper. Roll into a 3 cm diameter log, then wrap in baking paper and chill in the refrigerator.

- Meanwhile, bring beetroot to the boil in a saucepan of salted water. Reduce heat to low and cook for 50 minutes or until tender. To test whether they are cooked, insert a sharp knife into the largest beetroot; if it inserts easily they are ready. Drain beetroot, refresh in a bowl of cold water, then leave to cool slightly before slipping the skins off by hand; it's easier to do this while they are still a little warm. Cut into thin slices widthways, transfer to a baking tray and set aside.

- Preheat fan-forced oven to 180°C (350°F).

- Heat a char-grill pan or barbecue grill-plate as hot as possible. Remove kangaroo fillets from marinade, then season well with salt and pepper. Quickly sear in the char-grill pan or on the barbecue grill-plate for 2 minutes on the first side, then turn and cook for 1 minute; roo is at its best served rare so be sure not to overcook. Leave kangaroo to rest in a warm place for 5–10 minutes.

- Stack one-quarter of the beetroot slices in 1 or 2 piles on each of 4 plates, spreading a little of the anchovy butter between the slices as you go. Place plates in the oven for 3 minutes. Cut 4 thick discs from the remaining anchovy butter (the rest can be frozen for later use).

- Thickly slice kangaroo fillets on the diagonal, then divide among the warmed plates. Top kangaroo slices with a disc of anchovy butter, then dress rocket with a little olive oil and vino cotto and serve alongside.

Pan-roasted Saltwater Barramundi with Caramelised Lemon and Rocket

unsalted butter, for cooking

extra virgin olive oil, for cooking

4 × 160 g barramundi fillets, skin-on and pin-boned

sea salt and freshly ground black pepper

squeeze of lemon juice

rocket leaves, to serve

CARAMELISED LEMONS

½ cup caster sugar

1 cup water

3 lemons, 2 cut into 5 mm thick slices, and 1 juiced

2 teaspoons finely grated ginger

1 teaspoon finely chopped lemon thyme

SERVES 4

This recipe does not use the farmed plate-sized barramundi, but the ones caught in the wild and usually sold cut into fillets. Wild barramundi has a great flavour and texture, but you must take care when cooking it as it is a really dense-fleshed fish that needs to be cooked through. The caramelised lemon is a real sweet-sour concoction; adding the fresh ginger and lemon thyme at the last minute really balances its flavour beautifully.

◆ For the caramelised lemons, place sugar and water in a small saucepan and bring to the boil over medium heat, stirring until sugar dissolves. Increase heat to high and boil rapidly for 5 minutes or until a syrup begins to form. Reduce to lowest heat possible (use a simmer mat, if necessary), then add sliced lemons and juice and cook for another 10-15 minutes or until lemon slices are translucent and still hold their shape, taking care that the syrup does not darken in colour and caramelise. Remove from heat, then add ginger and lemon thyme and leave to infuse until required.

◆ Heat a knob of butter and splash of olive oil in a frying pan over medium-high heat. Season barramundi fillets with salt and pepper, then place in hot pan, skin-sides down, and cook for 4-5 minutes or until skin is crisp. Tip excess butter out of pan and add a little more butter, then carefully flip fish over and cook for another 4-5 minutes or until just cooked through and firm to the touch.

◆ Add a squeeze of lemon juice, then serve pan-fried barramundi topped with caramelised lemons (including a little of the syrup) and a rocket salad to the side.

Salmon Baked with a Stuffing of Pine Nuts, Currants and Preserved Lemon Wrapped in Vine Leaves

¼ cup dried currants

½ cup verjuice

¼ cup pine nuts

½ red onion, finely chopped

1 tablespoon finely chopped chervil

2 small quarters preserved lemon, flesh removed, rind rinsed and finely chopped

1 small bulb fennel, 2 tablespoons shaved, remainder sliced

50 g unsalted butter

1 × 800 g salmon fillet, centre-cut (not the tail end), pin-boned and halved lengthways

10–12 preserved vine leaves rinsed and dried

sea salt and freshly ground black pepper

extra virgin olive oil, for drizzling

VERJUICE BUTTER SAUCE

4 golden shallots, thinly sliced

1 cup verjuice

½ teaspoon sea salt

2 tablespoons double cream

220 g cold unsalted butter, chopped

freshly ground black pepper

lemon juice (optional), to taste

SERVES 4–6

I use vine leaves a lot in my cooking, simply because I am surrounded by grape vines at my farm. Even in winter, I keep a jar of preserved vine leaves on hand, although they must be soaked before using as the salt in the preserving mixture is very strong.

This is a good dish to serve at a dinner party – it's a little more work and has that special air of going to a lot of trouble about it. Although I do keep salmon fillets in the freezer for last-minute meals (see the recipe for Crisp-skin Salmon with Frozen Pea Salsa on page 116), I would only use a fresh piece for this dish.

The verjuice butter sauce is a wonderful addition to the salmon. It can be made in advance and kept warm in a thermos flask so there is no last minute pressure. It will solidify if left to go cold, but will still taste great nonetheless.

- Cover currants with verjuice, then leave to soak overnight or use a microwave set to the lowest power level for 5 minutes. Drain, reserving verjuice.

- Preheat fan-forced oven to 180°C (350°F).

- Place pine nuts on a baking tray and roast for 5–8 minutes or until golden, then set aside to cool. Reduce the oven temperature to 120°C (250°F).

- Mix together pine nuts, drained currants, onion, chervil, preserved lemon, shaved fennel and half of the butter.

- Place remaining fennel in a small roasting pan.

- Place the vine leaves, slightly overlapping, in a rectangle on a chopping board; make sure the rectangle is large enough to encase the salmon. Place the first piece of salmon, cut-side up, on top of the vine leaves and season well with salt and pepper. Pack the pine nut and currant mixture on top, then cover with the second piece of salmon, cut side-down. Season again, then carefully wrap into a parcel to completely encase with the vine leaves. Tie with kitchen string, then place salmon parcel on top of fennel in the pan.

- Add reserved verjuice, remaining butter and a drizzle of olive oil to the pan, then bake for 50 minutes, turning halfway through cooking. Baste salmon with pan juices once or twice during this time. If the fennel is not cooked, transfer the salmon to a large plate to rest, upside down, for 10 minutes, then return the pan to the oven, increase temperature to 200°C (400°F) and cook until fennel is tender and caramelised.

- Meanwhile, for the verjuice butter sauce, heat shallots, verjuice and salt in a small saucepan over medium-high heat until reduced to 2 tablespoons. Add cream and keep warm. Reduce heat to low, then add butter, a little at a time, returning pan to heat and whisking after each addition, taking care not to boil. Season to taste with salt and pepper, then add lemon juice, if using, to taste. Strain and discard shallots and keep sauce warm.

- Reheat salmon quickly in the oven just before serving, if necessary. The salmon should be only just set in the centre; if you have a meat thermometer it should register 46.9°C (116.4°F) when inserted in the thickest part.

- Cut off and discard kitchen string, then cut salmon into thick slices and serve with a drizzle of olive oil, with verjuice butter sauce and roasted fennel passed separately.

Barley Risotto with Asparagus and Fresh Goat's Curd

3 bunches asparagus

1 litre water

sea salt

60 g unsalted butter, chopped

extra virgin olive oil, for cooking

2 large leeks, white parts only, cleaned and sliced

1 cup pearl barley

½ cup verjuice

⅓ cup freshly grated Parmigiano Reggiano

120 g goat's curd

chopped flat-leaf parsley, freshly ground black pepper and lemon wedges, to serve

SERVES 4

I love the nuttiness of pearl barley and often use it when making a stuffing for lamb, kid or poultry. Using it to make a 'risotto'-style dish was an easy bridge for me to cross. Making a stock with the asparagus bases keeps it completely vegetarian. If you can't find fresh goat's curd simply replace it with ricotta, mascarpone or a large amount of grated pecorino or Parmigiano Reggiano instead. Don't forget to add loads of freshly chopped flat-leaf parsley and a squeeze of lemon juice at the end.

♦ Trim 4–5 cm from bases of asparagus. Roughly chop bases and set aside. Slice the tips off the asparagus, then slice the stalks into 2 cm lengths on the diagonal and set aside.

♦ Place chopped asparagus bases in a medium-sized saucepan, add water and a pinch of salt and bring to the boil. Cook over medium heat until asparagus is quite soft but still bright green in colour. Leave to cool slightly, then purée asparagus and water in a blender (or use a stab-mixer and purée in the pan). Reheat asparagus stock, then keep warm.

♦ Heat half of the butter and a splash of olive oil in a large, heavy-based deep frying pan or saucepan over medium heat, then add leeks and cook for 6–8 minutes or until tender but not coloured. Add barley and stir to coat with the leek mixture, then deglaze the pan with verjuice. Add hot asparagus stock a cupful at a time, stirring continuously and waiting for each cup to be absorbed before adding the next, for about 20 minutes or until barley is still a little crunchy. Season generously with salt and add sliced asparagus stalks and cook for another 10 minutes, then add asparagus tips. Cook for another 10 minutes or until asparagus is just coloured, continuing to add stock a cupful at a time. Add remaining butter and grated Parmigiano Reggiano and stir until melted.

♦ Divide risotto between 4 plates or bowls, then top each one with a generous spoonful of goat's curd, a final flourish of olive oil and grinding of black pepper. Squeeze with a little lemon juice, then serve immediately, scattered with lots of freshly chopped flat-leaf parsley.

Boston Baked Beans

500 g dried cannelini beans, soaked overnight in plenty of cold water

2 tablespoons mustard powder (I use Keen's)

¼ cup treacle

¼ cup soft-brown sugar

2 cloves

1 large onion, halved

100 g smoked pork belly, rind removed and cut into large pieces

2 fresh bay leaves

extra virgin olive oil, for cooking

1 × 400 g tin chopped roma tomatoes

¼ cup red-wine vinegar

sea salt and freshly ground black pepper

1 tablespoon chopped mint

SERVES 6-8

The exact cooking time of this dish will depend on the quality and age of the beans used; it can take around four hours for the beans to become tender.

- Drain and rinse beans, then place in a large saucepan, cover with water and slowly bring to the boil. Simmer gently over low heat for 45 minutes (use a simmer mat if necessary), then drain and leave to cool.
- In a bowl, combine mustard powder and 1 tablespoon of water to make a paste, then add treacle and brown sugar.
- Preheat fan-forced oven to 140°C (285°F).
- Insert 1 clove into each onion half, then place in a large, ovenproof heavy-based saucepan, casserole or deep-frying pan with smoked pork belly, bay leaves and a splash of olive oil and cook over medium heat for 5 minutes. Add tomatoes and mustard mixture and stir to combine. Add reserved beans, then cover with a tight-fitting lid or foil and bake for 4 hours or until beans are tender, stirring occasionally. Remove the lid for the last 30 minutes of cooking and add red-wine vinegar. Season to taste with salt and pepper
- When the beans are ready, add chopped mint and taste, then adjust seasoning, if necessary. If you find that the beans are too sweet, add a little more red-wine vinegar, then serve.

Stuffed Oven-baked Squid

extra virgin olive oil, for cooking

2 onions, finely chopped

2 cloves garlic, finely chopped

1 tablespoon rinsed and finely chopped preserved lemon rind (ordinary lemon zest would be fine too)

4 anchovy fillets, drained and finely chopped

½ cup fresh breadcrumbs (I like to use sourdough)

⅓ cup finely chopped flat-leaf parsley

4 small-medium squid tubes (about 8cm long), cleaned

sea salt

lemon wedges, to serve

SERVES 4

Squid is one of those ingredients that either must be cooked over high heat for the shortest possible time (think less than a minute) or long and slow using a low heat. As a result, the flavour of the squid is 'brighter' and fresher. We are so spoilt in the Barossa as for the majority of the year fishermen, from the Gulf of St Vincent, come up to our weekly Saturday growers' markets, bringing sweet, tiny Gulf prawns and the tenderest small squid (a by-product of prawning), already cleaned and ready to use. Without a doubt, they're the best squid I've ever eaten.

- Heat 2 tablespoons olive oil in a frying pan over medium heat. Sauté onion quickly for 5 minutes, then add garlic, lemon rind and anchovies and heat through. Add breadcrumbs, stir to combine, then remove from heat and add parsley.
- Preheat fan-forced oven to 200°C (400°F).
- Spoon one-quarter of the breadcrumb mixture into each of the cleaned squid tubes, filling them to about 2.5 cm from the ends. Skewer ends of tubes closed with toothpicks to prevent stuffing from spilling out.
- Place squid on a baking tray, drizzle with olive oil and season with salt, then bake for 3½-5½ minutes on each side, depending on the size of the squid.
- Transfer cooked squid to a plate and leave to rest. Remove toothpicks and drizzle pan juices over squid, then serve with lemon wedges alongside.

Pot-roasted Lamb Shoulder with Green Olives, Almonds and Apricots

½ cup blanched almonds

2 kg lamb shoulder, boned and cut into 4-5 cm pieces (ask your butcher to do this)

plain flour, for dusting

sea salt and freshly ground black pepper

extra virgin olive oil, for cooking

1 onion, finely chopped

2 cloves garlic, finely chopped

½ teaspoon chopped thyme

¾ cup dried apricots

1 litre lamb or chicken stock, as required

1 teaspoon chopped rosemary

¼ cup green olives, pitted

verjuice or dry white wine, for cooking

1 teaspoon finely chopped orange zest

freekeh (roasted green wheat), (see recipe page 20), or couscous with chopped flat-leaf parsley, to serve

SERVES 6-8

The shoulder and neck are definitely the sweetest parts of the lamb. Whilst cooking meat on the bone is my first preference, there are times when the advantage of boned and cubed meat means that the dish can go straight to the table from the oven or stove for everyone to serve themselves from the pot, rather than needing to worry about carving. This is certainly my preferred way to serve a meal for guests, especially when I'm organised enough to have the dessert or cheese course already prepared; once I've put the food on the table it is up to everyone else to serve and later help clear and, more importantly, wash up!

- Preheat fan-forced oven to 180°C (350°F).
- Place almonds on a baking tray and roast for 10 minutes or until golden. Leave to cool.
- Reduce oven temperature to 160°C (325°F).
- Toss lamb pieces in flour seasoned with salt and pepper, shaking to remove excess flour.
- Heat a splash of olive oil in a large frying pan over high heat, then, working in batches, cook the meat for 5 minutes or until golden on all sides. Remove and set aside.
- Heat a splash of olive oil in a cast-iron casserole over medium heat, then sauté onion, garlic and thyme for 5 minutes or until translucent. Add lamb pieces, apricots and stock to the pan (if using a Le Creuset, only add half of the stock), then cover with a tight-fitting lid and cook in the oven for 75-90 minutes or until the lamb is really tender. Remove lamb, cover with plastic film and keep warm. Cook pan juices over high heat until reduced and syrupy.
- Just before serving, heat another splash of olive oil in a small frying pan over medium heat, then add rosemary and fry for 30 seconds or until fragrant. Add olives and almonds and cook for another 1-2 minutes. Deglaze pan with a splash of verjuice or white wine, then add mixture to lamb. Stir in orange zest and season to taste with salt and pepper.
- Serve pot-roasted lamb with freekeh or couscous with chopped flat-leaf parsley stirred through.

Meatloaf with Tomato Sugo

500 g sausage mince (or you could use a half each mixture of minced beef or lamb with pork)

¼ teaspoon freshly ground black pepper

1 teaspoon sea salt

¼ cup tomato sugo (see recipe below) or Maggie Beer Pasta Sugo with Basil

¼ cup barbecue sauce

¼ cup Maggie Beer Cabernet Table Sauce or Chinese plum sauce

1 tablespoon worcestershire sauce

1 onion, finely chopped

2 tablespoons freshly chopped mixed herbs (such as marjoram, flat-leaf parsley and thyme)

1 free-range egg

plain flour, for dusting

TOMATO SUGO

20 g unsalted butter

2 tablespoons extra virgin olive oil

1 large onion, finely chopped

2 cloves garlic, finely chopped

⅓ cup red-wine vinegar

1 × 410 g tin chopped Italian tomatoes

1½ teaspoons caster sugar

1½ teaspoons sea salt

freshly ground black pepper

SERVES 4

Comfort food again. To me, meatloaf requires lots of sauces and chutneys from the larder to be truly delicious. The meat mixture also needs to be mixed by hand or it just doesn't taste the same. Sometimes I add slow-roasted tomatoes to the top of the meat during the cooking process. And sometimes I add dried porcini mushrooms to the mixture for extra depth of flavour. If you'd like to try this, cover 80 grams dried porcinis with verjuice and reconstitute them in the microwave on its lowest setting for 5 minutes, then chop and mix in with the other ingredients.

Although I usually serve meatloaf hot, any leftovers make a great lunch the next day, thickly sliced and placed in a brown bread sandwich with some pickles.

- For the tomato sugo, heat butter and olive oil in a saucepan over low heat, then add onion and garlic and cook, stirring occasionally, for 10 minutes or until caramelised. Increase heat to high, then add vinegar and reduce until evaporated. Add tomatoes, then return to the boil and cook for 3 minutes. Add sugar and salt and season with pepper, then reduce heat to medium and cook for 5 minutes. Reduce heat to low and gently simmer for another 15 minutes or until sauce thickens and most of the liquid has reduced. Set aside until required, then warm gently before serving.

- Preheat fan-forced oven to 180°C (350°F).

- Mix all the ingredients, except flour, together in a large bowl by hand. Shape mixture into a rectangle, then roll to coat in flour and place in a loaf tin. Press down firmly.

- Bake meatloaf for 40 minutes or until cooked through. If you have a meat thermometer the internal temperature should be 70°C (158°F). Leave to rest.

- Serve thick slices of meatloaf topped with spoonfuls of the warmed tomato sugo.

Whole Roasted Red Onions with Buffalo Mozzarella and 'Pulled' Bread

⅓ cup extra virgin olive oil, plus extra for cooking

1 large clove garlic, chopped

4-6 slices stale bread such as sourdough or ciabatta, crusts removed and torn into long pieces

8 large red onions, unpeeled

sea salt and freshly ground black pepper

⅓ cup vino cotto

1 tablespoon thyme leaves

320 g buffalo mozzarella, divided into 8 pieces

rocket leaves, to serve

SERVES 4

I have a passion for vegetables especially, as I'm sure I've said already, when they come straight from my own garden. Mind you, if my crop fails, I know the local farmers' market will provide. Onions are so incredibly sweet, and when they are baked and drizzled with vino cotto they could easily be the centrepiece of a meal in their own right. I wanted to include buffalo mozzarella in this dish, having recently visited Victoria's Shaw River Buffalo Cheese dairy, where I helped to stretch the hot curds with a partner to form the mozzarella balls. There is nothing quite like getting in and being part of the process and I feel so privileged to have had the chance. My biggest tip for cooking with fresh mozzarella in a hot dish such as this is to add it in the last few minutes of cooking, otherwise it will be tough.

- Preheat fan-forced oven to 200°C (400°F).
- Pour olive oil into a small container, then add garlic and process with a stab mixer or (pound with a mortar and pestle) until a paste forms. Place bread on a baking tray, then pour over oil mixture and rub it into bread. Bake for 10-12 minutes or until crisp and golden, then set aside.
- Reduce oven temperature to 180°C (350°F). Rub whole onions with olive oil, salt and pepper, then place in a baking dish that is just big enough to hold them snugly in 1 layer. Drizzle vino cotto evenly over onions and sprinkle with half of the thyme. Roast onions for 60-90 minutes or until tender. Peel skin from the tops back a little and use a small, sharp knife to cut a criss-cross in the onion tops, pulling the sides away to create a 'crater'. Top each onion with some of the 'pulled' bread, the remaining thyme and 2 pieces of mozzarella. Return to the oven for 3-4 minutes or until mozzarella has melted.
- Serve onions immediately with a rocket salad to the side.

Macaroni Cheese

1.2 kg jap or Queensland blue pumpkin, peeled, seeded and cut into small chunks

4 stalks rosemary, leaves picked and chopped

sea salt

extra virgin olive oil, for cooking

¼ cup verjuice

2 litres milk

2 fresh bay leaves

160 g unsalted butter, chopped

160 g plain flour

1 tablespoon freshly grated or ground nutmeg

250 g grated Parmigiano Reggiano

400 g large macaroni

150 g Persian goat's feta, crumbled

250 g grated cheddar

SERVES 12-16

My mother often made this rich and luscious dish when we had relatives coming to dinner. Now when I think about the small oven she had to work with, it makes sense that she chose to bake a dish that took maximum advantage of the limited space available. Mum never wrote down a recipe in her life, so I only have the memory of what she did to go by. I remember that, even when I was a child, she'd use the sharpest possible cheese she could find (in those days it was a New Zealand Epicure cheese). I have contributed my own touch, adding roasted pumpkin and Persian feta. It definitely needs to be served with a bitter leaf salad alongside; my stock-in-trade one is made with radicchio, rocket and witlof, dressed with a good vinaigrette (see the dressing on page 176).

* Preheat fan-forced oven to 200°C (400°F).

* Line a baking tray with baking paper, then add pumpkin and rosemary, season generously with salt and drizzle with olive oil. Roast for 30 minutes or until pumpkin is tender and starting to brown. Take tray out of oven, then drizzle verjuice over pumpkin. Return tray to oven and cook until verjuice has evaporated.

* Meanwhile, heat milk with bay leaves in a saucepan over high heat until almost boiling, then remove from heat and leave to infuse for 10 minutes. Remove and discard bay leaves and keep milk hot.

* Melt butter in a saucepan over medium heat until nut-brown. Add flour and cook until flour and butter come together, stirring for several minutes. Remove from heat and slowly pour in hot milk, using a whisk to incorporate and prevent any lumps forming. Return to the heat and stir with a wooden spoon for another 10 minutes or until the sauce is shiny and coats the back of the spoon. Add nutmeg and grated Parmigiano Reggiano, stirring continuously until the cheese has melted. Taste the sauce to see if any salt is necessary; take care to only season with salt after you've added the grated Parmigiano Reggiano as it can be salty enough. Cover the surface of sauce closely with plastic film to stop a skin from forming and set aside until needed.

* Cook macaroni in a large saucepan of boiling salted water until al dente, then drain and place in a large mixing bowl. Add the cheese sauce to the macaroni and mix through well, then add the pumpkin and toss through gently. Gently stir in the crumbled feta. Transfer the macaroni mixture to a large 2.5 litre baking dish (mine is a 40 × 30 × 5 cm), top with grated cheddar and bake for 10-20 minutes or until brown.

* Serve immediately.

Quince-glazed Quail

40 g quince paste

½ cup water

squeeze of lemon juice

extra virgin olive oil, for cooking

1 small onion, finely chopped

3 super-thin slices round pancetta, finely chopped

1 tablespoon finely chopped rosemary

50 g unsalted butter, chopped

100 g chicken livers

¼ cup pine nuts

30 g fresh white breadcrumbs

sea salt and freshly ground black pepper

6 jumbo quail (about 200 g each)

rocket leaves (optional), to serve

SERVES 6

When cooked this way, quail just melts in the mouth. Although some find quail to be a bit small, this is such a rich dish that all but those with the largest of appetites would be satisfied with just one quail per person, particularly considering the luscious stuffing. I seek out the jumbo quail from the Game Farm in New South Wales. I like to serve these quail with grilled polenta to the side, but soft polenta (see recipe page 103) or even just boiled waxy potatoes such as my favourites, nicolas, would be fine too. A salad of bitter greens such as witlof, radicchio and rocket would be the perfect accompaniment.

It may seem like a lot of trouble to brown the stuffed quail in butter before painting them with the quince glaze, but the results make it well worth the extra effort.

- Melt quince paste with the water and lemon juice in a small saucepan over low heat, stirring until the mixture becomes smooth and lump-free. Take care not to burn the paste. Set aside.

- Heat a splash of olive oil in a frying pan over low-medium heat, then sauté onion, pancetta and rosemary for 6-8 minutes or until just tender. Transfer to a bowl and set aside.

- Heat half of the butter and a splash of olive oil in the same pan over medium-high heat. When butter foams, add livers and cook for about 1 minute on each side or until they are just coloured on the outside but still pink on the inside – be careful when adding livers to the pan as they have a tendency to 'spit'. Remove from the pan and leave to cool slightly. Trim livers, then cut into large pieces and discard any connective tissue and add to the onion mixture. Add pine nuts and breadcrumbs and gently stir to combine.

- Preheat fan-forced oven to 220°C (450°F).

- Season the cavity of each quail with salt and pepper. Divide breadcrumb mixture equally between the quail and carefully fill each cavity. Tuck wings underneath the quail. If you want to, you can secure the quail legs together with a toothpick or tie with kitchen string (see opposite) – this prevents the stuffing from spilling out while the quail cook. Season quail with salt.

- Heat the remaining butter in a clean large frying pan over medium heat, then, when it's foaming, add quail to the pan and gently brown on all sides. Place the quail on a baking tray, breast-sides up, then brush the quince glaze generously over each quail; if the glaze is too hard to spread, then gently reheat it over low heat.

- Roast the quail for 10-12 minutes or until cooked through; do not overcook. Leave to rest, breast-sides down, in a warm place for 10-15 minutes before serving.

- Serve quail on a bed of rocket leaves, if desired.

Beef Pie Mix

1 kg beef chuck (I use Coorong Angus beef), cut into 1.5 cm cubes
(or 2 cm cubes for 1 large pie)

gluten-free flour, for dusting

sea salt and freshly ground black pepper

extra virgin olive oil, for cooking

50 g tomato paste

2 cloves garlic, crushed

100 g golden shallots or small pickling onions, halved lengthways

150 g sugar-cured bacon, roughly chopped

600 ml shiraz

150 g portobello or button mushrooms, trimmed and roughly chopped

2 cups veal or chicken stock

2 fresh bay leaves

1 teaspoon finely chopped thyme

GLUTEN-FREE PASTRY

2 cups water

1 tablespoon salt

180 g unsalted butter, chopped

300 g gluten-free flour, plus extra for dusting

4 g xanthum gum (available from health food stores and large supermarkets)

5 free-range eggs

MAKES 10 INDIVIDUAL PIES OR
1 LARGE PIE

This beef pie is not one you could ever buy, no matter how good the baker. For me, the only way to make a beef pie is to start with a great piece of beef (even when using a secondary cut). Of course, the shiraz helps too, adding a terrific shine, as does the flavour boost of the bacon and mushrooms.

Here I've used a choux-style gluten-free pastry, which I love because it browns beautifully, has a nice crisp finish and holds moisture in well. Ready-made gluten-free flour is available from large supermarkets and health food stores, but I like to mix my own. I use equal quantities of potato flour, rice flour and maize flour. The addition of potato flour gives the pastry a pleasant potato undertone. It also keeps well in the refrigerator for up to five days. To use it for sweet pies, simply add 2 teaspoons of icing sugar when you add the flour, if desired.

- Toss beef cubes in flour seasoned with salt and pepper to just coat (I find using a plastic bag is good for this). Heat a splash of olive oil in a heavy-based saucepan over high heat, then brown beef in 3-4 batches until golden.

- Reduce heat to medium and return all the beef to the pan, then stir in tomato paste and garlic and cook for 1 minute. Add shallots and bacon, then season with salt. Increase heat to high and add red wine to deglaze the pan. Add mushrooms and stock and bring the mixture to the boil, skimming off any impurities that rise to the surface. Add bay leaves and thyme.

- Cover and cook beef over low heat for 2½-3 hours or until it is tender. Check seasoning and add pepper. Remove the meat with a slotted spoon, then reduce sauce over high heat until it thickens. Return the meat to the pan and stir to combine. Leave to cool until needed. The pie mix can easily be made a day or two in advance and kept in the refrigerator.

- Meanwhile, for the gluten-free pastry, combine the water, salt and butter in a heavy-based saucepan. Bring to a simmer over medium-high heat, then add flour and xanthum gum. Stir vigorously with a wooden spoon, then decrease heat to low and cook until the pastry comes away from the side of the pan and is well combined. Remove from the heat and cool to room temperature.

- Whisk eggs, then slowly stir a little of the beaten eggs at a time into the cooled flour mixture with a wooden spoon until a dough forms, incorporating each addition fully before adding the next bit; you may not need to use all of the eggs.

- Turn dough out onto a bench dusted with gluten-free flour, then knead until shiny. Try not to incorporate too much of the extra flour or the dough will become crumbly. Wrap the dough in plastic film and chill in the refrigerator for at least 10 minutes.

- Preheat fan-forced oven to 210°C (425°F).

- Roll the pastry out to 3 mm thick between 2 sheets of greased baking paper (otherwise the dough is too hard to handle). Cut the pastry into 20 rounds slightly larger than your pie tins, then use half to line the bases and sides of the pie tins.

- Add cooled beef pie filling to pastry cases, then top with remaining pastry rounds, pressing around edges to seal. Bake pies for 20 minutes or until pastry is golden. Serve at once.

Tuna Confit with Vine Leaves

2 tablespoons roughly chopped
flat-leaf parsley

2 tablespoons roughly chopped basil

sea salt

1 × 900 g piece tuna, centre-cut and
bloodline removed

6 large fresh grape leaves, blanched
and dried or 6 preserved vine leaves,
rinsed and dried

extra virgin olive oil (not the most
expensive one), for cooking

3 golden shallots, thinly sliced

6 small ripe tomatoes, roughly chopped

4 stalks thyme

finely grated zest of ½ lemon

VINAIGRETTE

⅓ cup fruity green extra virgin olive oil

1 tablespoon lemon juice

sea salt and freshly ground black pepper

SERVES 6

I have been making a version of this recipe for the past twenty years or so, ever since first enjoying it at Gay Bilson's acclaimed former restaurant, Berowra Waters Inn. I've tried to recreate the dish, using my palate memory as a guide. Then, after recently reading Janni Kyritsis' wonderful cookbook, *Wild Weed Pie*, I discovered that Janni's secret to this dish was to leave the tuna to cool in the olive oil used for poaching; this makes an amazing difference to the finished result as it just becomes so incredibly moist. I've incorporated Janni's advice into my method.

You will need to start making this the day before you plan to serve it. As the tuna is served at room temperature, it is an ideal dish to prepare when catering for a party as all the work is done in advance.

- Preheat fan-forced oven to 150°C (300°F).
- Combine parsley, basil and 2 tablespoons salt, then rub into the tuna. Wrap tuna in vine leaves and place in an ovenproof loaf tin or terrine mould that is just large enough to hold the tuna, shallots and tomatoes.
- Heat 2 tablespoons olive oil in a saucepan over medium heat, then add shallots, tomatoes and thyme and sauté for 8-10 minutes or until shallots are translucent. Add lemon zest and stir to combine.
- Pour shallot and tomato mixture over tuna in loaf tin or terrine mould, then add enough olive oil to immerse the tuna completely. Bake tuna for 35 minutes.
- Remove tin from the oven and insert a thin metal skewer into the centre of the tuna. Test the skewer by pressing it against your bottom lip; if the tuna is ready the skewer should feel just warm. If the skewer feels cool, then return tin to the oven for another 5-10 minutes. Leave tuna to cool in the poaching oil, then refrigerate in the oil overnight.
- The next day, take the wrapped tuna out of the oil. Strain the poaching oil, reserving the shallot and tomato mixture. The strained oil can be refrigerated and kept for a few weeks for other uses such as cooking fish – I would not recommend using it for salad dressings as refrigeration will alter its character.
- For the vinaigrette, mix fruity olive oil and lemon juice, then season with salt and pepper to taste. Add reserved shallot and tomato mixture and stir to mix.
- Cut vine-leaf wrapped tuna into thick slices. Spoon the vinaigrette over the tuna and serve at once.

Turkey with Apple and Prune Stuffing and Glazed Chestnuts

1 × 10 kg corn-fed, free-range turkey, wing tips removed and reserved

50 g unsalted butter, softened

sea salt

1 onion or apple, for holding the stuffing in place

1 tablespoon plain flour (optional)

APPLE AND PRUNE STUFFING

100 g dried apples, roughly chopped

200 g prunes, pitted

150 ml verjuice

½ cup extra virgin olive oil

2 large onions, finely chopped

⅓ cup sage, roughly chopped

unsalted butter, for cooking

180 g chicken livers

⅓ cup flat-leaf parsley, roughly chopped

2 tablespoons rosemary, roughly chopped

2 tablespoons thyme, roughly chopped

2½ cups fresh breadcrumbs

65 g thin slices prosciutto, chopped

sea salt and freshly ground black pepper

GLAZED CHESTNUTS

500 g frozen peeled chestnuts

2 cups chicken stock, plus 1 litre extra (optional)

extra virgin olive oil, for cooking

1 onion, roughly chopped

½ cup verjuice or dry white wine

SERVES 16–20

Can I admit that I had never cooked a turkey before coming up with this recipe? Turkey isn't part of my family's traditional Christmas fare, and, when offered it by others, I used to request the stuffing and pass on the bird, having only experi-enced dry meat with little flavour. But what a difference using a corn-fed, free-range turkey makes – luckily for me, Colin raises about six hundred of these a year. An even bigger surprise was the success of using an oven bag – it resulted in such a moist and luscious bird that it converted me immediately.

However, a ten kilogram turkey is too big for an oven bag. But if you are preparing this for Christmas dinner at the same time as you are glazing a leg of ham, then the ham skin can be placed over the turkey to help keep it moist during cooking or use a piece of muslin soaked in melted butter. These are just two of the many tips I've received from kind viewers of my show since it began.

I make this with frozen peeled Australian Chestnut Company chestnuts, which can be purchased online (cheznutz.com.au). It is so convenient to have a stockpile of these on hand in my freezer for occasions when I want to use peeled chestnuts – especially when they are not in season.

If you prefer, the dried apple in the stuffing can be replaced with two peeled, cored and chopped granny smith apples.

- For the stuffing, reconstitute dried apples in half of the verjuice for 10 minutes or until soft, then drain. Reconstitute prunes in the remaining verjuice for 10 minutes, then roughly chop. Heat olive oil in a frying pan over medium heat, then sauté onions for 10 minutes or until translucent, adding the sage just before removing the pan from the heat. Transfer to a bowl and set aside.

- Heat a knob of butter in the pan over high heat, then sear chicken livers for 2 minutes on each side or until golden on the outside but still pink in the centre. Remove pan from the heat and leave the livers to rest for 5 minutes, then remove any connective tissue and cut them into large chunks.

- Preheat fan-forced oven to 180°C (350°F).

- In a large bowl, combine the herbs, breadcrumbs, onions, livers, apples, prunes and prosciutto, then season to taste with salt and pepper. If the stuffing doesn't hold together when you squeeze it, add some warm olive oil or butter to bind it. Fill turkey cavity with the stuffing mixture, then massage the softened butter into the breast, sprinkle with salt and use an onion or apple to hold the stuffing inside the cavity.

- If the turkey fits into an oven bag, then place the flour in the bag and shake to coat, tipping out any excess. Carefully slide turkey into the bag, then tie the end with kitchen string and slip the bag into another oven bag, then seal with kitchen string again. Bake in a roasting pan for 2 hours.

- Carefully open the bags, collect any juices that have collected by pouring them into a tall jug, then refrigerate to solidify the fat, making it easier to remove. Increase oven temperature to 200°C (400°F), then return the turkey to the roasting pan and roast for another 30 minutes to brown.

- Alternatively, if the turkey is too big to fit into a large oven bag, then place a piece of baking paper (or a piece of muslin soaked in melted butter) over the breast to help retain moisture. Roast for 40 minutes, then reduce oven temperature to 120°C (250°F) and roast for another 2½ hours or until cooked through and the juices run clear when the thickest part of the thigh joint is pierced with a skewer.

- Meanwhile, for the glazed chestnuts, simmer chestnuts and stock in a saucepan over low heat for 20 minutes or until tender. Drain chestnuts, reserving the stock. Heat a splash of olive oil in a saucepan over high heat, then sauté the reserved turkey wings and chopped onion. Deglaze the pan with verjuice or white wine, then add the reserved chestnut stock, 1 litre of either reserved turkey pan juices with fat removed if you used an oven bag, or chicken stock or water. Cook over high heat for 10 minutes or until reduced and syrupy. Strain the sauce, then add the chestnuts and warm through.
- Serve the turkey on a large platter, with the stuffing and glazed chestnuts to the side (or you can pour the glazed chestnuts over the turkey).

Slow-cooked Berkshire Pork Shoulder in Milk

1 × 2 kg shoulder of pork, skin-on and boned (ask your butcher to do this)

extra virgin olive oil, for cooking

¾ cup verjuice or white wine

3 cups full-cream milk

4 fresh bay leaves

sea salt and freshly ground black pepper

SALT MIX

¼ cup fennel seeds

½ cup sea salt

finely grated zest of 1 lemon

4 stalks lemon thyme, leaves picked

SERVES 6-8

This is one of those dishes I'd read about and always wanted to cook, and when I finally used the principle of braising meat in milk, I was astounded by the flavour. I, of course, wanted to add verjuice as I'm always searching for that sweet-sour balance. The sauce curdles, but it is meant to, and this does not detract from its flavour. Whilst this is not a pretty dish, what it lacks in the looks department it more than makes up for in flavour.

You'll need to get started on this the day before you plan to serve it as the pork benefits greatly in flavour and texture from being salted at least eight hours or preferably overnight before cooking. Because the pork is braised in milk there won't be any crackling, but the skin will be soft, gelatinous and, to my mind, particularly delicious. As the pork is so rich, I like to serve it with bitter greens such as a rocket, witlof and radicchio salad alongside.

- For the salt mix, dry-roast fennel seeds, sea salt, lemon zest and thyme in a small frying pan over low heat, tossing continuously until the mixture gives off a rich aroma; take care not to burn. Remove from heat and leave to cool.
- Using a very sharp knife (I like to use a Stanley box cutter), evenly score pork skin at 5 mm intervals, then score in the opposite direction to form a diamond pattern, taking care not to cut through to the meat. Stand pork in a large roasting pan, then pour boiling water over the skin. This helps the score marks to open up and release fat when the pork cooks (you may have to repeat this process if the score marks don't open up enough). Pat the pork dry with paper towels. Rub cooled spice mix generously into all sides of the pork, then cover with plastic film and refrigerate overnight.
- Next day, remove pork from the refrigerator at least 1 hour before cooking.
- Preheat fan-forced oven to 150°C (300°F).
- Wipe any excess salt mix from the pork with a paper towel. Heat a splash of olive oil over medium-high heat in a cast-iron casserole with a tight-fitting lid just large enough to hold the pork (my Le Creuset one is ideal for this). Add pork and brown on all sides, then deglaze pan with verjuice.
- In a saucepan, bring milk and bay leaves to simmering point over high heat. Pour warm milk and bay leaves into the pan with the pork, adding enough to come three-quarters of the way up the sides of the meat. Cover with the lid and bake for 4½ hours or until the pork is as soft as butter, basting the meat occasionally with pan juices. The milk will curdle but don't be put off as it will still be absolutely delicious.
- Transfer pork to a large plate, then cover with foil and leave to rest. Carve into thick slices, then spoon the sauce over and season to taste with salt and pepper.

Chocolate Ganache Tart with Blood Orange

TART SHELL

125 g plain flour

100 g chilled unsalted butter, chopped

¼ cup sour cream

CHOCOLATE GANACHE

1 cup double cream

250 g dark couverture chocolate
(70 per cent cocoa solids), chopped

10 g unsalted butter

BLOOD ORANGE CONFIT

⅓ cup caster sugar

⅓ cup water

2 blood oranges, thinly sliced

juice of 1 lemon

SERVES 8–10

I absolutely love blood oranges; they're such a winter treat. I never tire of freshly squeezed blood orange juice for breakfast or added to a glass of Campari later in the day, and I also love to cook in sugar syrup and serve them with a rich chocolate tart. I make more blood orange confit than is needed for this recipe as I enjoy serving it as a sweetmeat with a cup of strong espresso or sometimes I even dip them into melted chocolate for an after-dinner treat.

Unless you have couverture chocolate (see page 16) there is no point in making this tart. And the trick of pouring hot cream over chopped chocolate to melt it is one well worth knowing – not only is it incredibly easy but it also gives a beautiful sheen to the finished dish.

- For the blood orange confit, bring sugar and water slowly to the boil over low heat, stirring constantly until the sugar dissolves. Leave to cool.
- Preheat fan-forced oven to 150°C (300°F).
- Lay orange slices in a baking dish so they overlap slightly. Pour over cooled syrup and cover with baking paper and foil. Bake orange slices for 1 hour, then remove foil and baking paper and return to the oven to cook until the syrup is thick and orange slices are caramelised; this can take another 30–60 minutes. Squeeze lemon juice over to give the syrup a glossy sheen. Store in the refrigerator for up to 1 month.
- For the tart shell, process flour and butter in a food processor until mixture resembles coarse breadcrumbs. With the motor running, gradually add enough of the sour cream to help the pastry just come together to form a ball. Turn out onto a lightly floured bench and bring together into a rectangle with your hands. Wrap in plastic film and chill in the refrigerator for at least 20 minutes.
- Preheat fan-forced oven to 220°C (450°F).
- Roll out pastry, then gently place over a 22 cm tart tin with a removable base, pressing pastry into the side of the tin and leaving an overhanging border. Line pastry with foil, fill with pastry weights or dried beans and blind bake (see page 16) for 12 minutes, then trim pastry to edges of the tin. Remove foil and weights and bake for another 5 minutes. Leave tart shell in the tin on a wire rack to cool.
- For the chocolate ganache, bring cream to the boil in a heavy-based saucepan over medium heat. Place chocolate in a heatproof bowl and pour over boiling cream. Set aside for 3 minutes, then stir to melt the chocolate. Add butter to the warm chocolate mixture to give the ganache a shiny finish. Pour ganache into the cooled tart shell and refrigerate until set; it should not take more than 1 hour.
- Place slices of the blood orange confit in the centre of the tart then cut into slices and serve.

Meyer Lemon Curd and Raspberry Jelly Trifle

¾ cup pouring cream, lightly whipped

¼ cup sweet sherry

1 × 400 g tin peaches without added sugar (I use a jar of my own preserved peaches, but tinned ones are fine too)

RASPBERRY JELLY

300 ml unsweetened raspberry juice (available from delicatessens)

60 g caster sugar

3.5 × 2 g gelatine leaves

MEYER LEMON CURD

4 free-range egg yolks

⅔ cup caster sugar

3 teaspoons finely grated meyer lemon zest, plus 100 ml strained lemon juice

GÉNOISE SPONGE

5 free-range eggs, at room temperature, separated

¾ cup caster sugar

150 g plain flour

60 ml melted clarified unsalted butter (see page 59)

SABAYON

¼ cup sangiovese verjuice or white wine

¼ cup caster sugar

4 free-range egg yolks

SERVES 4–6

Who doesn't like trifle? Each component of this trifle is so special, from the simple but delicious sabayon to the homemade raspberry jelly. You will need to make the jelly the day before serving to give it time to set. The real hero is the Meyer lemon curd, which we make by the bucketful every May, when meyer lemons are at their most abundant and best; this recipe makes about 300 ml and any extra will keep, once opened, in the refrigerator for up to three months.

I use homemade preserved peaches, now made for me by my friend Sherry Schubert as I no longer have the time to do it myself. It is fine to use tinned Aussie peaches instead, just choose ones with no added sugar. I assemble this about an hour before my guests are due to arrive. Any leftovers will still be delicious the next day, but the texture will be quite different.

- For the raspberry jelly, bring raspberry juice and sugar slowly to the boil in a saucepan over low heat, stirring frequently to dissolve sugar. Set aside and leave to cool slightly. Meanwhile, put gelatine leaves in a bowl with enough cold water to cover and leave to soften for a couple of minutes. Squeeze excess water out of gelatine leaves and drop them into the just-warm raspberry juice mixture, stir well, then pour into a shallow 1 litre baking dish and place in the refrigerator overnight to set. Cut into bite-sized cubes.

- For the meyer lemon curd, whisk egg yolks and sugar in a large stainless steel bowl until frothy, taking care not to over-beat. Transfer to a heavy-based stainless steel saucepan and add remaining ingredients, then stir continuously over low heat to combine for 10–15 minutes or until mixture thickens and coats the back of a wooden spoon; if you have a sugar thermometer the temperature should be 82°C (179–180°F). Transfer immediately into a hot sterilised jar if not using that day, then seal and store for up to 3 months. Otherwise, place a round of baking paper on the surface to prevent a skin from forming and leave to cool in the refrigerator.

- For the génoise sponge, preheat fan-forced oven to 190°C (375°F). Grease and line a 26 cm cake tin. Beat egg whites to soft peaks with hand-held electric beaters, then beat in caster sugar a tablespoon at a time until the mixture is stiff and all the sugar has been absorbed. Place yolks in a bowl and lightly whisk. Gently stir one-quarter of the egg white mixture into the yolks, then pour the yolk mixture over the remaining egg white mixture. Sift the flour on top and then carefully fold it in. Fold in cooled clarified butter to make a batter. Pour batter into the prepared tin and bake for 25 minutes or until the cake begins to come away from the side of the tin and feels springy. Cool on a wire rack.

- For the sabayon, heat verjuice or wine and sugar in a heavy-based saucepan over low heat until sugar has dissolved. Place egg yolks in the stainless steel bowl, then whisk in the warm verjuice or wine and sugar mixture until light and frothy. Place the bowl over a saucepan of simmering water and continue to whisk until mixture is pale and thick; do not allow water to boil. Do not let the base of the bowl touch the water. To check if the consistency is right, lift the whisk out of the bowl; you should be able to make a trail of the number eight with the mixture. Remove from the heat and continue to whisk until cool. Refrigerate until needed.

- To assemble the trifle, gently fold half of the lightly whipped cream into the sabayon. Remove and discard crusts from sponge, then cut cake into large pieces (I use a 1.5 litre bowl), then lay a piece of sponge in the bottom of your serving dish; the size depends on the dish you use. Spoon over a little sherry, then spread with a layer of lemon curd. Place peach slices on top of the curd, then spoon over some sabayon and top with jelly cubes. Repeat this layering process a few times until all the ingredients have been used. Top the final layer with the remaining whipped cream and cubes of jelly, if desired, cover loosely with plastic film and refrigerate until ready to serve.

- Spoon the trifle into bowls, then serve.

Baked Vanilla Custard with Coffee Jelly

1 cup pouring cream

½ cup milk

1 vanilla bean, split lengthways

5 free-range egg yolks (using 60 g eggs)

70 g caster sugar

⅓ cup seville orange marmalade

140 ml strong black coffee or espresso
(I use 2 double short blacks with the
crema removed, but a good-quality
instant coffee would also work, with
a little sugar added if necessary)

1 × 2 g gelatine leaf

whipped cream and raspberries
(optional), to serve

SERVES 4

Many years ago I had a similar dish at an excellent Italian restaurant in London. They baked and chilled the custard in cappuccino cups, and as orders for it came in, they made a *ristretto* (strong shot of) coffee and poured it over, then served it immediately. Upon returning home I played with the idea, putting it on the menu of an ill-fated restaurant Colin and I once ran with friends in Adelaide, where it was a huge hit. The concept of turning the coffee component into a jelly came about when putting together the restaurant's first Valentine's Day menu for two, so coffee wouldn't need to be made at the last minute, spoiling the rhythm of the meal – that was the idea then, anyhow!

It is best to make the custard the day before so it has time to set, then add the coffee jelly on the day you plan to eat these.

- Preheat fan-forced oven to 160°C (325°F).
- Bring cream, milk and vanilla bean to the boil in a small heavy-based saucepan over high heat, then remove from the heat and leave to infuse for 15 minutes.
- Using hand-held electric beaters, beat egg yolks and sugar together until thick and pale.
- Scrape the seeds from the vanilla bean into the cream mixture and reheat over high heat until hot. Pour the hot cream mixture over the egg yolk and sugar mixture and stir until all the sugar has dissolved.
- Place 1 tablespoon of marmalade in the base of four 250 ml ovenproof coffee cups.
- Pour one-quarter of the custard mixture through a fine sieve (this eliminates the froth) into the four cups, then place in a roasting pan and fill halfway with boiling water. Bake custards for 35–40 minutes or until they are set but still a little wobbly in the middle. Remove from oven and leave to cool in the water bath. When the custards have cooled, put them in the refrigerator to chill overnight.
- The next day, make the coffee and leave to cool slightly; it still needs to be warm enough to dissolve the gelatine. If you have a really sweet tooth you could add a little sugar to the coffee, however the custard has sugar so, to me, the dish is already sweet enough.
- Soak gelatine leaf in cold water for a few minutes until it softens. Once soft, squeeze out the excess liquid from the gelatine and add to the tepid coffee, then stir to dissolve. Remove any crema on top of the coffee as you want the surface of the jelly to shine. Let coffee and gelatine mixture cool a little, then carefully divide half of the coffee mixture among the chilled custards and leave to set for 10 minutes. Divide remaining coffee mixture among the cups, then return to the refrigerator and leave to set for at least 1 hour. (Doing this in stages helps to achieve the shiny mirror-like effect on the surface of the jellies.)
- Top with spoonfuls of whipped cream and serve with raspberries to the side, if desired.

Chocolate, Almond and Prune Slab

100 g blanched almonds

100 g pitted prunes

50 ml Oloroso or other sweet sherry

200 g dark couverture chocolate
(70 per cent cocoa solids), chopped

⅓ cup double cream

20 g unsalted butter, chopped

SERVES 8

This is such a simple treat. I really enjoy great chocolate after a meal, and this easy recipe fits the bill. I'm a real prune lover too, but years of running a restaurant and developing food products have shown me that they just don't sell. So from here on, when working on new ideas for my product range, I'm going to call them exactly what they are – dried plums. Of course, if you really dislike prunes you could use the same amount of raisins instead, but the lusciousness of prunes is my definite choice here.

Make the slab a couple of hours before you need it, and once it is set, break it into irregular pieces so that everyone knows that you made it yourself. Be sure to take the slab out of the refrigerator a little while before serving as it tastes so much better when it is not icy cold.

- Preheat fan-forced oven to 200°C (400°F).
- Place almonds on a baking tray and roast for 10 minutes or until golden, then leave to cool and roughly chop.
- Soak prunes in sherry until all the liquid is absorbed, then roughly chop.
- Place chopped chocolate, cream and butter in a heatproof bowl over a saucepan of simmering water, and cover the bowl with plastic film (this prevents steam or moisture getting to the chocolate, as contact with water can make the chocolate seize or become grainy and hard to melt and combine).
- Fold chopped prunes and almonds through the warm chocolate mixture, stirring to combine.
- Line a baking tray with baking paper and pour in the chocolate mixture, then spread it evenly into a slab. Cover with plastic film and refrigerate for about 1 hour or until set.
- Break into irregular shapes and sizes for a truly homemade effect and then serve as a sweetmeat with coffee or glasses of dessert wine. Once set, store in a sealed airtight container in a cool, dark cupboard, not in the refrigerator.

Ricotta, Honey and Pears

1 large round fresh ricotta
(the best that you can find)

4 ripe pears, cored

1 lemon

⅔ cup honey (such as leatherwood, mallee or chestnut), to serve

SERVES 8

The success of this dish, perhaps more so than any other, lies in the quality of each individual ingredient. It is only worth doing if you can buy excellent fresh ricotta, preferably directly from the maker like I am able to do in Adelaide (either from La Casa Del Formaggio or La Vera Mozzarella); it's even better if you manage to get it just after it's been made. Of course, then there is the honey to consider. Whilst I love to use imported Italian chestnut honey, if choosing an Australian honey I'd use a Tasmanian leatherwood, as I prefer more 'savoury' honeys such as these. This may sound like an oxymoron, but I find many honeys are just too sweet for me.

- Place ricotta round in the centre of a large round plate. Slice pears and squeeze with lemon juice so that they don't brown, then place around the ricotta. Pour a rich, gutsy honey over the top of the ricotta and serve immediately.

Meyer Lemon Posset

550 ml pouring cream

50 g caster sugar

finely grated zest of 2 meyer lemons, plus ½ cup lemon juice, strained

raspberries and whipped cream (optional), to serve

SERVES 8

I first tasted this wonderfully rich but light (yes that is possible) dessert when staying with our friends Peter and Amanda at their Hamptons home in the USA, for the 4th July holiday weekend. Colin and I arrived, jetlagged, from Australia in the afternoon, and they kindly had a car waiting to take us to this quite amazing part of America (indeed, the world). It was a real privilege to be invited to stay for the holiday weekend in a private home where food, wine and art were definitely passions we shared with our hosts. Ever since, this dessert, (which I now know has British origins) has become a real favourite of mine.

Meyer lemons have a thinner, more vibrantly yellow skin than their more common counterparts, lisbon lemons, and they are also slightly sweeter, which is why I prefer to use them for this. If you can't get hold of meyer lemons, then use the more usual variety and adjust the flavour by adding an extra 50–100 grams of sugar, depending on how sweet you like things.

- Combine cream, sugar and lemon zest in a small heavy-based saucepan. Bring to the boil, then boil for 3 minutes. Pour into a bowl and leave to cool.
- When cream mixture is cool, using hand-held electric beaters, whisk the strained lemon juice into the cream mixture, aerating it as much as possible, until soft peaks form; you should have a 'soft-whip' texture. Pour into eight 125 ml cups or moulds and chill in the refrigerator for at least 4–5 hours or overnight.
- Serve lemon posset with raspberries and whipped cream, if desired.

Baked Apples

50 g unsalted butter, at room temperature, chopped

⅓ cup soft-brown sugar

2 tablespoons roughly chopped almonds

½ teaspoon ground cinnamon

½ teaspoon finely grated lemon zest

4 clusters dried muscatels, 2 with muscatels left on the stems and 2 picked

4 granny smith apples

2-4 tablespoons verjuice or riesling

double cream, to serve

SERVES 4

The recipe for this childhood favourite came about thanks to a recent visit to Adelaide's historic Carrick Hill Estate to see their wonderful orchard. They've spent a lot of time and resources in bringing the orchard back to life and it now boasts more than seventy heritage apple varieties. When the time came to picking an apple variety to cook with, it was a little daunting, so I took the advice of Carrick Hill's Director, Richard Heathcote, and chose the more sharply flavoured gooseberry pippin, as one of their characteristics is that they almost 'melt' when cooked. As I adore the juxtaposition between sweet and sour flavours, I loved using these apples as they suit my palate; so much so that I even committed to grafting some of their bud wood over with one of my apple trees when the timing was right. It was such a treat to have access to an heirloom apple variety, but for the rest of the time, the granny smith does very well for making a stuffed baked apple.

- Preheat fan-forced oven to 180°C (350°F).
- Process butter, sugar, almonds, cinnamon, lemon zest and half of the picked muscatels in a food processor until blended. Transfer to a bowl and add remaining picked muscatels, stir to combine, then set aside.
- Use an apple corer to remove the apple cores and create a cavity, but don't push through to the base of the apples. Use a teaspoon to scoop out any remaining cores to create a good-sized cavity and maximise the room for holding the stuffing. If the apples don't sit upright, slice across their bases to make them flat. Divide butter mixture between apple cavities, then place them in a baking dish. Add whole muscatel clusters to the dish, then pour verjuice or riesling over both muscatels and apples.
- Bake apples and muscatels for 1 hour or until the apples are soft, caramelised and luscious. Serve with cream.

Cheddar, Quince and Walnut Mille-feuille

100 g walnuts

plain flour, for dusting

375 g purchased all-butter puff pastry (I use Carême)

150 g crème fraîche

100 g extra-sharp cheddar, finely grated (I use Mersey Valley)

80 g quince paste, chopped

SERVES 8

My friend Marg Lehmann, of Peter Lehmann Wines, asked me to come up with a cheese course with a twist to be paired with Lehmann's Mentor Shiraz Cabernet for a dinner in October 2007 at the Grand Hyatt hotel in Melbourne. I've never been one to advocate that red wine automatically goes with cheese, thanks in part to my indoctrination by noted cheese authority Will Studd of the Calendar Cheese Company. However, I've always maintained that if a match between the two were to be made, it would have to include a sharp or aged cheddar. Marg and I tossed around ideas as we sat at her Barossa kitchen table, and this dish is the result.

It requires an extra-sharp cheddar, and I find that Mersey Valley Vintage Club Classic works really well here as it crumbles naturally. The walnuts could easily be replaced with almonds. I am lucky to have ready access to Carême butter puff pastry, made here in the Barossa. If you can't get hold of it, do search out a frozen product made with butter, as it will make all the difference to the final result. This dessert is rich, so I'd recommend serving it after a simple meal.

- Preheat fan-forced oven to 180°C (350°F).
- Place walnuts on a baking tray and roast for 10 minutes, checking frequently to make sure they don't burn. Immediately wrap in a clean tea towel, then rub to peel off skins. Sift rubbed walnuts through a sieve to get rid of skins, then leave to cool. Roughly chop cooled walnuts and set aside.
- Lightly dust a bench with flour, then roll out pastry. Place pastry on a baking tray lined with baking paper. Prick all over with a fork and refrigerate for at least 20 minutes.
- Increase oven temperature to 220°C (450°F). Bake pastry for 20 minutes or until golden. Remove from oven and leave to cool. Cut pastry into 16 strips, approximately 10 cm × 5 cm.
- Combine crème fraîche and cheddar, stirring to form a paste. Spread crème fraîche mixture on 8 strips of pastry, then top with walnuts and quince and sandwich together with remaining pastry strips, pressing down gently, then top with more crème fraîche mixture, walnuts and quince to form 8 mille-feuille.
- Place mille-feuille in oven for 5 minutes or until the cheese begins to melt. Serve warm.

Rhubarb Crumble

1 large bunch (about 1 kg) ripe rhubarb, leaves discarded and stems washed and cut into 4 cm pieces (discard any brown bits)

½ cup caster sugar or ¼ cup honey

finely grated rind and juice of 2 oranges, plus extra juice as needed

125 g plain flour

1 teaspoon ground cinnamon

⅓ cup dark-brown sugar

100 g rolled oats

140 g chilled unsalted butter, chopped

double cream, to serve

SERVES 4

Because I love rhubarb, I have eight large rhubarb 'crowns' growing in my garden, although I now wish I'd planted a range of varieties. The rhubarb I grow is deep ruby-red and rather delicious, but recently I came across one of the growers at the local Saturday Barossa Farmers' Market who grows a pale-green variety, which, he says, is a little sweeter than my more traditional variety. I found this quite fascinating as I don't like to add a lot of sugar when cooking rhubarb, so I'd be really happy to have a variety on hand that requires even less sugar than I use now.

When making this crumble I often cook double the amount of rhubarb and keep the extras in the refrigerator. I especially enjoy having a big spoonful of cold rhubarb, along with a splash of runny cream swirled around it, on my porridge in winter – all healthy of course!

If you want to cook the rhubarb and crumble together from the onset, toss the rhubarb with a little of the orange juice and the zest and sugar, then place in a baking dish and cover with the remaining orange juice. Scatter the crumble mixture on top and bake for 1 hour.

- Preheat fan-forced oven to 180°C (350°F).
- Spread rhubarb in a baking dish, sprinkle with caster sugar or honey and orange juice and bake for 20 minutes or until tender, then set rhubarb and pan juices aside. Add a little extra orange juice if there are no juices left in the dish.
- Combine flour, cinnamon, sugar, orange zest and oats, then rub the butter into the flour using your fingertips.
- Place cooked rhubarb and pan juices in a buttered 1 litre ovenproof dish or four 250 ml ramekins, sprinkle with crumble, then bake for 15 minutes (for ramekins) or 25 minutes (if baking in one dish) or until golden.
- Serve crumble in bowls with double cream passed separately.

Chocolate and Hazelnut Roulade

175 g dark couverture chocolate
(70 per cent cocoa solids), chopped

6 free-range eggs, separated

175 g caster sugar

60 g plain flour (optional)

2 tablespoons icing sugar

2 tablespoons unsweetened
dutch-process cocoa powder,
plus extra to serve

crème fraîche, to serve

FILLING

200 g hazelnuts

1 cup crème fraîche

1 × 200 g jar Nutella

SERVES 8

The premise behind my cooking is to focus on seasonal ingredients, basing what I cook on what is in season at the time. Here, the star of the recipe is the fresh Australian hazelnuts, which I roasted and rubbed of their skins – the difference between these and their imported counterparts, sold with no indication of their year of harvest, is nothing short of incredible. I also had in my mind the need to also use readily accessible products so I've used Nutella as it too is made from hazelnuts; the fact that it is so sweet lead me to balancing this with the beautiful acidity of crème fraîche.

I'm always a little nervous when making something a bit tricky in the desserts department, so with the help of Dianne Wooldridge, a wonderful country cook who works at the farm, I created this relatively fuss-free take on a roulade. Recipes for chocolate roulade often don't contain flour, but I've included it here as an optional addition, because it helps to prevent the cake from cracking badly when it is rolled.

I think this roulade is best served at room temperature as something in its flavour is lost when refrigerated.

- Preheat fan-forced oven to 180°C (350°F). Line a lightly greased swiss roll tin with baking paper or a silicone baking mat.

- Melt chocolate in a heatproof bowl placed over a saucepan of simmering water (make sure the chocolate doesn't come into contact with any steam and that the base of the bowl doesn't touch the water) or in a microwave on high for 4 minutes, then leave to cool slightly.

- Beat egg yolks and sugar with hand-held electric beaters until mixture is pale and frothy. Sift and fold in flour, if using. Fold in the slightly cooled melted chocolate.

- Whisk egg whites with clean hand-held electric beaters until soft peaks form, then carefully fold them into the chocolate mixture in 3 batches so that the egg whites don't collapse (I find that a large metal spoon is ideal for this).

- Spread mixture evenly over the base of the swiss roll tin, then bake for 15–20 minutes or until the sponge is firm on top but still soft to touch.

- Meanwhile, mix icing sugar and cocoa together and sift onto the middle of a clean tea towel that is slightly larger than the swiss roll tin.

- Remove swiss roll tin from the oven, then carefully turn the cake out so that it is on the centre of the icing sugar and cocoa-dusted tea towel (I place the shortest side of the swiss roll tin at a 45° angle to the tea towel on the bench, then quickly flip it upside down over the tea towel). Carefully peel away the baking paper or silicone sheet. Working quickly while the cake is still hot, gently roll up from the short side of the tea towel, using the edge of the rolled towel as a guide. Leave the cake to cool in the rolled position for about 15 minutes.

- For the filling, roast hazelnuts at 180°C (350°F) for 5 minutes. Rub their skins off, then roughly chop a little. Mix crème fraîche and Nutella together, then fold in chopped hazelnuts and set aside.

- Carefully unroll the cake, then spread filling over the sponge, leaving a 2 cm border. Re-roll the cake, making sure that the first roll is very tight (about 2 cm wide). Don't worry if the sponge cracks in places – it looks more appetising and real that way. Dust generously with cocoa powder and leave for a few hours in a cool place for flavours to meld.

- Serve slices of roulade at room temperature, topped with an extra dollop of crème fraîche.

Passionfruit Parfait

1 cup coconut milk

100 ml pouring cream

4 free-range egg yolks

90 g caster sugar

150 ml passionfruit pulp
(from 8-10 passionfruit)

MAKES ABOUT 1 LITRE

This recipe is inspired by Martin Boetz of Longrain restaurant, a talented Sydney chef and a truly lovely person. I first met him years ago when I cooked at a fund-raising dinner for breast cancer research in Sydney. My friend Alex Herbert (who worked at the Pheasant Farm restaurant during its last six months) arrived on the night with Martin in tow and we each had to cook a course for three hundred people – a tall order at any time, but the camaraderie made it fun and helped us to get through it. Ever since, I've followed Martin's career. I took inspiration for this directly from him, but added some changes of my own so it can be made without an ice cream machine. Thank you Martin!

* Bring coconut milk and cream to the boil in a heavy-based saucepan, then set aside.
* Beat egg yolks and sugar with hand-held electric beaters until pale and thick, then pour coconut and cream mixture over egg mixture and whisk until combined. Pour mixture into a clean heavy-based saucepan and heat it gently over low heat, stirring with a wooden spoon for a few minutes or until it coats the back of the spoon. Don't allow the mixture to boil as it will curdle. Pour the mixture into a bowl and chill in the refrigerator overnight.
* Stir passionfruit pulp into the chilled mixture, then transfer to a 1 litre baking dish, place in the freezer and leave to freeze. Stir occasionally so that the custard becomes creamy and frozen without forming lumps.
* Serve scoops of parfait in bowls or glasses.

Coeur à la Crème

2 tablespoons caster sugar

6 heads unsprayed lavender, roughly chopped

300 g fresh ricotta (try to find an unsalted one) or gruth (a fresh, unripened cheese made in the Barossa)

100 g mascarpone or sour cream

¼ cup mixed candied citrus peel

500 g frozen mulberries, slightly thawed or 500 g fresh strawberries

1 × quantity Sugar Syrup (see recipe page 27)

SERVES 4

In the days when I ran my restaurant, the Pheasant Farm, I had twenty-four of the traditional ceramic heart-shaped coeur à la crème moulds with holes in the bases for draining the liquid from the cheese overnight. I misplaced them and subsequently mourned their loss, until a former colleague phoned me to say he had closed his restaurant and offered me his.

I guess I'm a bit of a romantic as I feel using the heart-shaped vessel adds so much to the final dish. Although many recipes for coeur à la crème use a combination of cream cheese and sour cream, I always loved preparing this dish most in the restaurant when a local producer made fresh curd or cottage cheese without salt for me. Now, I prefer to use ricotta or locally made gruth (a fresh, unripened soft cheese similar to quark), especially when I can organise to get some without salt, as this maximises the sweet flavour of the dish.

- Combine sugar and lavender with a mortar and pestle until the lavender has been completely pounded and its essential oils have been released into the sugar.
- Mix ricotta and mascarpone together, then stir in the sugar and lavender mixture and mix well. Stir in citrus peel to combine.
- Line a large coeur à la crème mould (or 4 small ones) with a large clean piece of muslin or Chux, then spoon in the ricotta mixture, cover with overhanging muslin or Chux and leave on a tray to catch the drained liquid to set in the refrigerator overnight.
- Place mulberries and sugar syrup in a stainless steel saucepan and cook over medium heat for 2 minutes. Remove mulberries with a slotted spoon and set aside, then simmer syrup over high heat until reduced and syrupy.
- Carefully remove coeur à la crème from the mould/s, place gently on a plate and carefully peel off the muslin or Chux.
- Serve coeur à la crème with mulberries and a little syrup to the side.

Chocolate and Dried Pear 'Brownie'

300 g dark couverture chocolate (70 per cent cocoa solids), chopped

250 g unsalted butter, chopped

4 free-range eggs

2 free-range egg yolks

200 g soft-brown sugar

60 g plain flour, sifted

40 g dutch-process cocoa powder, sifted, plus extra for dusting

2 cups plump, moist dried pears, chopped (if pears are a bit dry, hydrate in verjuice for 10 minutes before using)

CRÈME FRAÎCHE PARFAIT (OPTIONAL)

3 cups crème fraîche or sour cream

1½ cups caster sugar

¾ cup water

6 free-range egg yolks

SERVES 6-8

This recipe began as a pursuit for the best brownie ever and eventually morphed into a pudding. Whilst I've made it with the beautifully plump and moist dried pears that I buy from Margaret Ellis at the Saturday Barossa Farmers' Market, I've also made it to great effect with glacé cumquats (come to think of it, dried figs would be good too).

It's important to note that the cooking vessel used will have a dramatic effect on the cooking time. The first time I made it I used a ceramic bowl that I chose for its lovely shape as I thought it would be great to take straight from the oven to the table, but it took nearly an hour to cook. Alternatively, it might take only 25 minutes to cook in a cake tin. This is such a reminder that the timing can depend on differing factors such as ingredients, ovens and, in this case, cooking vessels.

- For the crème fraîche parfait, if making, whip crème fraîche or sour cream with an electric mixer until soft peaks form, then cover with plastic film and refrigerate. Place a 1 litre baking dish into the freezer to chill.

- Heat sugar and water in a small saucepan over low heat, stirring continuously until sugar dissolves. Brush down side of the pan with a wet pastry brush to prevent crystals forming. Cook syrup until it reaches 'soft ball' stage. (That is, the stage when a spoonful of syrup will form a smooth, pliable ball when dropped into a glass of iced water, then removed and rolled into a ball between your fingertips. This can also be tested by checking the syrup with a sugar thermometer; it should read 115°C [241°F]). Remove from heat immediately.

- Beat egg yolks in a clean bowl with hand-held electric beaters, then pour sugar syrup over in a steady stream, continuing to beat mixture at medium speed until it cools to room temperature. Once cooled, fold mixture into whipped cream, then pour into the chilled baking dish, cover with plastic film and freeze overnight.

- Preheat fan-forced oven to 180°C (350°F).

- Melt chocolate and butter in a heatproof bowl placed over a saucepan of simmering water (make sure the chocolate doesn't come into contact with any steam and that the base of the bowl doesn't touch the water) or in a microwave on high for 4 minutes. Stir to completely combine the melted butter and chocolate, then leave to cool a little.

- Beat together eggs, egg yolks and sugar in an electric mixer until thick and pale; when you run the spatula through the mixture, a trail should remain. Stir in the cooled chocolate mixture, then fold in sifted flour and cocoa, followed by pears.

- Grease a large baking dish (I use a 20 cm soufflé dish but a cake tin would work too), then pour in the mixture and bake for 30 minutes. Reduce oven temperature to 160°C (325°F) and cook for another 15–20 minutes, depending on how gooey you like it in the middle and the size and material of the cooking vessel you use. The pudding will rise up and then sink and crack a little. The surface should be springy in the centre and a spoon should come out only slightly sticky when inserted.

- Serve 'brownie' dusted with extra cocoa powder, with scoops of crème fraîche parfait to the side, if desired.

Sicilian Rice Pudding

2 cups flaked almonds

1.5 litres milk

⅔ cup caster sugar

2 cups short grain calrose rice
(don't use arborio)

40 g unsalted butter

½ teaspoon ground cinnamon

1 cup mixed candied orange and
lemon peel

1 tablespoon finely grated lemon zest

½ cup pouring cream, plus extra to serve

SERVES 6-8

Some years ago, Colin and I planned a trip to Sicily but, for various reasons that I can't even remember now the trip was postponed for what ended up being several years. Those were the days when I took time out to present classes on the circuit of the top cooking schools in Australia. Such commitments were often made six to twelve months in advance and I had undertaken to present a class on Sicilian food, based on my experiences in Sicily. While the trip hadn't eventuated, the commitment was still there, so I threw myself into researching every book about Sicilian food I could find. This recipe, with its Sicilian flavours, was one that really appealed to me, and my take on it has been part of my repertoire ever since.

- Preheat fan-forced oven to 180°C (350°F).
- Roast flaked almonds on a baking tray for 8-10 minutes or until golden brown, taking care not to burn them. Set aside to cool.
- Place milk, sugar, rice and butter in a large saucepan and stir over medium heat. Once rice has started to cook, mash it with a wooden spoon to break down some of the grains. Simmer rice gently over low heat for 40-50 minutes or until tender and creamy, stirring frequently to prevent it from sticking to the base of the pan.
- Remove from the heat, then add half of the almonds, cinnamon, candied peel and lemon zest. Stir in cream to combine, then transfer to a large serving dish, scatter with remaining almonds and serve at once with a jug of pouring cream to the side.

Chestnut Purée Dessert

1 × 439 g can unsweetened
chestnut purée

½ cup pouring cream

¼ cup verjuice or water

20 g unsalted butter, chopped

30 ml Cognac

2 tablespoons seville orange marmalade

CHOCOLATE GANACHE

100 ml pouring cream

100 g dark couverture chocolate
(70 per cent cocoa solids), chopped

10 g unsalted butter

SERVES 8

Chestnuts seem to be an ingredient that really polarise people. I for one love their strange sweet nuttiness and find lots of uses for them in addition to simply roasting them over an open fire, while Colin finds them dry and absolutely hates their floury texture. Luckily for those who fall into my camp, Australian chestnut growers have started producing frozen peeled chestnuts for specialty food stores and local chestnut farmers sell dried chestnuts and even sometimes fresh chestnut flour. I also must confess, though, to sometimes buying cans of imported French chestnut purée as a matter of convenience, which I have used here. However, if this delightful dessert appeals to you and you are looking for a way to use Australian chestnuts, then you could always start from scratch and cook, peel and purée one kilogram of fresh chestnuts (or cook and purée the frozen variety) to make your own.

- Place chestnut purée, cream and verjuice or water in a saucepan, then cook, stirring over low heat for 5 minutes or until combined. Add butter, then stir until melted and combined with other ingredients. Stir in Cognac.
- Remove from heat, then purée in a food processor until smooth. Divide purée evenly among eight 125 ml cups and refrigerate for 20 minutes or until firm.
- For the chocolate ganache, bring cream to the boil in a heavy-based saucepan over medium heat. Place chocolate in a heatproof bowl and pour over boiling cream. Set aside for 3 minutes, then stir to melt the chocolate. Stir butter in to warm chocolate mixture to give it a shiny finish.
- Top each cup with 1 teaspoon marmalade, then cover with warm ganache.
- Refrigerate desserts until set, then serve.

My Version of Pashka - an Easter Dessert

½ cup chopped crystallised ginger

½ cup dried currants

¼ cup mixed candied citrus peel

¼ cup chopped dried figs

¼ cup chopped dried pear (about 1 slice)

2 tablespoons Galliano Amaretto

½ cup slivered almonds

100 g unsalted butter, chopped

½ cup caster sugar

2 free-range egg yolks

finely grated zest of 1 lemon,
plus 2 tablespoons juice

finely grated zest of 1 orange

750 g fresh ricotta

½ cup sour cream

fresh or dried fruit, to serve

SERVES 8

Whilst I was delighted with the flavour of a pashka I made for my television show, I have since altered the recipe slightly after an encounter with some viewers for whom pashka is a family tradition more than a recipe. They called in to the Farm Shop on their way to Adelaide to show me a beautifully carved wooden pashka mould that was part of their family's food culture and told me their traditional way of making this dessert. I've learnt so much in my time with this show and love the fact that people feel comfortable in sharing their food knowledge with me - it was just one of the many times when viewers have had an impact on what I do.

• Line a 2 litre bowl with a piece of muslin or a clean damp Chux, ensuring it hangs over the edge of the bowl.

• In a separate bowl, combine ginger, currants, candied peel, figs and pear with the Amaretto, then leave to infuse for 2 hours.

• Preheat fan-forced oven to 180°C (350°F).

• Place almonds on a baking tray and roast for 8-10 minutes or until golden, then remove and leave to cool.

• Cream butter and sugar with an electric mixer until pale and thick, then add egg yolks, one at a time, and beat in well. Add grated citrus zests and ricotta and continue to mix well. Fold in soaked fruit mixture, lemon juice and roasted almonds, then fold in sour cream.

• Spoon mixture into the muslin-lined bowl, then cover with plastic film and refrigerate for at least 8 hours or overnight, tucking all the overhanging muslin into the bowl so that moisture doesn't leak down the sides.

• Carefully turn out pashka, then serve with fresh or dried fruit to the side.

Fruit Slice

1 × quantity Sour-cream Pastry
(see recipe page 92)

homemade vanilla bean ice cream
or Maggie Beer Vanilla Bean and
Elderflower Ice Cream, to serve

FRUIT MINCE

2 freshly grated granny smith or
pink lady apples (to yield 200 g)

100 g raisins

100 g candied orange peel

50 g soft-brown sugar

¼ teaspoon ground nutmeg

¼ teaspoon ground cloves

¼ teaspoon ground allspice

¼ teaspoon ground cinnamon

½ cup sweet sherry

200 ml verjuice

SERVES 6-8

In true country-cook style, I was looking for a way to use all the fruit mince
I had left over from making my Christmas puddings for the Farm Shop
when I came up with the idea for this. The result was so delicious, I set
about making fruit mince especially so that I could make this again – it
well and truly passed my test for whether I'd want to cook it again soon
with flying colours.

- Make sour-cream pastry according to instructions on page 92.
- For fruit mince, combine all ingredients in a saucepan, bring to a simmer
  over medium heat, then reduce heat to low and simmer for 1 hour or until
  all liquid has evaporated.
- Lightly grease a 38 × 24 cm baking tray and line with baking paper. Cut
  pastry into 2 portions, one just over half the amount of the pastry, then wrap
  the smaller piece in plastic film and chill in the refrigerator until required.
  Roll out the larger piece until 3 mm thick, forming a rectangle large enough
  to leave a 2 cm border of pastry overhanging the edges of the tray (the
  pastry will shrink). Place pastry onto baking tray, then prick with a fork.
  Cover with plastic film and refrigerate for 2 hours or place in the freezer
  for 15 minutes.
- Preheat fan-forced oven to 230°C (475°F).
- Bake pastry for 4 minutes, then remove from oven and use a clean tea towel
  to press down on the pastry to prevent it from bubbling up; take care not to
  burn yourself. Return to oven for another 2 minutes, then remove and leave
  to cool.
- Roll out remaining pastry until 3 mm thick, then cut into 6 mm wide strips.
  Set aside.
- Spread fruit mince evenly over cooled pastry. Top fruit mince with pastry
  strips, placing them in a criss-cross or lattice pattern. Cover with plastic
  film and refrigerate for at least 10 minutes.
- Bake for another 5 minutes or until lattice pastry is cooked and golden.
- Serve the warm slice topped with scoops of ice cream.

Sultana Cake

3 free-range eggs (using 55 g eggs)

150 g caster sugar

⅓ cup extra virgin olive oil

60 g unsalted butter, melted

75 ml milk

200 g plain flour

1 teaspoon baking powder

finely grated zest of 4 lemons

large pinch freshly grated or ground nutmeg

500 g picked fresh seedless green grapes (about 3 cups picked grapes)

1 tablespoon demerara sugar

icing sugar (optional), for dusting

fresh vine leaves (optional), to serve

SERVES 8-10

In 1994 a local women's group, the Soroptimist International of Barossa Valley Inc., produced *Riches from the Vine*, a soft-cover cookery book containing a great potpourri of recipes related to the grape, for which I had the honour of writing the foreword for. This cake takes inspiration from a recipe in the book, although given my inclination for generous flavours, I've added more grapes, more lemon – well, basically more of everything. The outcome is a cake that is so incredibly moist it lasts for days – that is if anyone has the strength of character to not keep going back for more.

With its beautiful crisp golden-brown exterior and luscious interior, this cake is absolutely tantalising eaten warm from the oven. So much so that it could easily double as dessert; just add a jug of caramel sauce and a swirl of cold pouring cream.

- Preheat fan-forced oven to 180°C (350°F).
- Grease and line a deep 20 cm springform cake tin with baking paper.
- Using hand-held electric beaters, beat eggs and sugar until pale and thick. Add oil, butter and milk and mix well.
- In a separate bowl, sift together flour and baking powder, then stir in lemon zest and nutmeg.
- Tip flour mixture into egg mixture and stir to combine. Add two-thirds of the picked grapes and stir to just combine, then pour into prepared cake tin and bake for 15 minutes. Remove from oven and sprinkle with remaining grapes and demerara sugar. Return to oven and bake for another 40 minutes or until a skewer inserted into the middle of the cake comes out clean.
- Turn cake out onto a wire rack and leave to cool.
- Dust cooled cake with icing sugar, if using, then cut into slices and serve on a bed of fresh vine leaves, if desired.

Almond Affogato

a few scoops of Maggie Beer Vanilla Bean and Elderflower Ice Cream or other good-quality vanilla bean ice cream

Galliano Amaretto, to taste

1 shot espresso coffee, with crema (I use a very small shot of coffee, called a *ristretto*, which is more concentrated and strongly flavoured)

SERVES 1

Affogato is such a simple thing to do that I wonder whether we even need a recipe for it at all – but I prefer to think of including it here as a way of jogging the memory – a reminder of how lovely it is to enjoy. I tasted my first ever affogato on a warm autumn afternoon in one of Rome's piazzas, and, as with so many of my food memories, every time I have it I am transported back to a special time or place. The almond component is provided by the Amaretto, which is my favourite liqueur for this. Like just about everything I make, the success of this dish is all about the strength of the individual ingredients. The *ristretto* (strong shot of espresso) is an absolute must. At the Farm Shop we serve affogato with my brand of Vanilla Bean and Elderflower Ice Cream, and this makes a world of difference again.

I seldom order dessert at a restaurant, but if I know they make a good coffee, and they have affogato on the menu, then I'm in like Flynn!

- Fill a tall glass with scoops of ice cream, pour over the Galliano Amaretto to taste, then pour over freshly made coffee. Enjoy at once.

Vanilla Bean Panna Cotta

3 cups thickened cream

1 plump vanilla bean

90 g caster sugar

3 × 2 g gelatine leaves

POACHED CHERRIES

½ cup verjuice

¾ cup caster sugar

½ cup water

60 cherries, stems attached

SERVES 6

You'll need to make this the day before you wish to serve it to allow the panna cotta to set in the refrigerator overnight. Sometimes I serve this with fresh mulberries or unrefrigerated ripe strawberries alongside, which you could do too if they are in season. Otherwise, I serve it as I've done here (see opposite), with cherries poached in a verjuice sugar syrup.

• Heat cream and vanilla bean in a saucepan over low heat. As cream starts to warm, remove vanilla bean, then halve it lengthways and scrape the seeds into the cream. Return pan to the heat, then slowly pour in sugar in a steady stream, stirring until it dissolves. Remove from heat and leave to cool a little.

• Meanwhile, place gelatine sheets to soften in cold water for 5 minutes, then squeeze to remove excess moisture. Stir soaked gelatine leaves into warm cream mixture until dissolved.

• Divide mixture among six 125 ml moulds. Cover with plastic film and leave to set in the refrigerator overnight.

• For the poached cherries, place verjuice, sugar and water in a saucepan and slowly bring to the boil over low heat, stirring continuously to dissolve sugar. Add cherries and cook for 10 minutes, then remove with a slotted spoon and set aside. Increase heat to high and simmer syrup for 6–8 minutes or until reduced to a glaze. Pour over cherries and leave to cool.

• Dip panna cotta moulds briefly in warm water, then turn out onto plates and serve with poached cherries and syrup to the side.

Golden Syrup Dumplings

1 cup self-raising flour, plus extra for dusting

pinch of salt

20 g unsalted butter

1 free-range egg, lightly beaten

50 ml milk

pouring cream, to serve

SAUCE

1½ cups golden syrup

½ cup water

60 g unsalted butter, chopped

SERVES 4-6

My memories of my mother making this dish goes back to when I was three or four years old. At the time we lived in Rose Bay, in Sydney, before our move to the Western suburbs. I seem to recall a prolonged blackout caused by a huge storm that was buffeting the sea one night when Mum made these. The electricity must have gone off at that crucial moment when the dumplings were being poached in the syrup, but I still remember Mum turning it into a special occasion as we ate the delectable dumplings by candlelight. The very smell (not to mention taste) of these dumplings takes me back to that evening, and the feeling of being warm and safe from the raging storm outside.

• Sift flour and salt into a bowl. Rub in butter with your fingertips, then add beaten egg and stir to combine. Slowly add milk, stirring until the mixture forms a stiff dough. Set aside.

• For the sauce, combine all ingredients in a large frying pan with a tight-fitting lid. Bring to the boil over high heat, stirring to combine, then reduce heat to low and simmer until reduced and syrupy.

• Meanwhile, lightly flour your hands and roll the dough into 3 cm balls (they will swell as they cook and, if any bigger than this, they will be dry in the centre), placing them on a plate lined with baking paper as you go. Slip the balls into the simmering syrup, then cover and cook for 10 minutes. Turn dumplings and cook for another 10 minutes.

• Remove dumplings with a slotted spoon, then serve topped with the sauce and with a jug of cream to the side.

Peanut Butter Pie

PIE CRUST

180 g wheatgerm crackers
(I use Arnott's Breton crackers)

90 g unsalted butter, melted

3 teaspoons caster sugar

FILLING

1 cup pouring cream

⅓ cup caster sugar

320 g cream cheese, chopped,
at room temperature

375 g crunchy salt-free peanut butter

TOPPING

150 ml double cream

150 g dark couverture chocolate
(70 per cent cocoa solids), chopped

20 g unsalted butter

SERVES 16

I can hardly believe that I love this tart so much – it has to be the richest dessert I've ever made. I should start off by confessing that peanut butter (of the crunchy, non-salty variety) has been a hidden vice all my life – so much so that I fear having a jar of it in the house because I know I'd finish it within days. Whilst the idea adding peanut butter to a pie may seem odd to some, it appealed to me.

This recipe came about when the South Australia Tourism Commission invited me to represent South Australia in a cooking challenge against California, to be held at an amazing ranch called Alisal in the Santa Ynez Valley. Cooking in a strange kitchen with different ingredients (not to mention the good-hearted rivalry) was an exhausting task, but one of the dishes that absolutely stood out to me was an incredible peanut butter and chocolate tart. Its creator, Alisal's executive chef, Pascal Gode, kindly shared the recipe with me. I've taken out a lot of the sugar and used an even more indulgent chocolate ganache than the original, resulting in a super-rich pie that probably needs a health warning before you eat it.

- Preheat fan-forced oven to 160°C (325°F).
- For the pie crust, process crackers in a food processor until crumbled. Combine crumbs with butter and sugar, then press into the base of a 22 cm springform cake tin and bake for 10 minutes. Set aside to cool.
- For the filling, simmer cream and sugar over low heat, stirring until sugar dissolves. Blend cream cheese and peanut butter in a food processor. Add cream mixture and pulse to combine, then spoon filling on top of pie crust and leave to cool.
- For the topping, bring cream to the boil in a saucepan over high heat, then remove pan from the heat. Place chocolate and butter in a heatproof bowl, then pour over hot cream and leave for 3 minutes without touching. Gently move dish around to melt chocolate and butter into the cream. Pour topping over pie, then refrigerate uncovered for 4 hours or until set.
- Once set, serve small slices of the pie – it is very rich!

Brown Sugar and Vino Cotto Parfait

100 g hazelnuts

270 g soft-brown sugar

400 ml double cream

30 ml vino cotto

5 free-range egg whites

pinch of ground cinnamon

Roasted Quince with Cinnamon and Orange (see recipe page 229), to serve (optional)

SERVES 6-8

Last autumn, during the height of quince season, I read a recipe by Skye Gyngell for a brown-sugar parfait, and as I'm always thinking about quinces, this sounded like a great thing to serve with them – I couldn't wait to try it. I totally neglected to read that Skye's recipe incorporated puréed quinces – how's that for synchronicity of flavour matches! I left the puréed quince out of my version, and served it with Roasted Quince with Cinnamon and Orange instead. Whilst Skye's version included sherry I used vino cotto instead, which made a beautiful addition. I also used our local Kernich's Jersey cream (but 45 per cent cream would be fine too); it gave such a rich and buttery result that everyone loved.

The challenge was to make the caramel for the parfait without using a sugar thermometer, as so few households seem to have one in their kitchen gadgets drawer.

- Preheat fan-forced oven to 180°C (350°F).
- Place hazelnuts on a baking tray and bake for 10 minutes, checking frequently to make sure they don't burn. Immediately wrap in a clean tea towel, then rub to peel off skins. Sift rubbed hazelnuts through a sieve to get rid of skins, then leave to cool. Roughly chop cooled hazelnuts and set aside.
- Place sugar and 140 ml of the cream in a small saucepan, then bring to the boil over high heat and boil for 2 minutes. Cool a little until a slight skin forms. Add vino cotto to cooled cream mixture and stir to combine.
- Lightly whip remaining cream until soft peaks form, then set aside; take care not to over-beat as it will split.
- Using a clean and dry electric mixer, beat egg whites until medium peaks form. Pour cream and sugar mixture immediately into egg whites, then use a spatula or large metal spoon to gently fold in whipped cream, cinnamon and hazelnuts.
- Transfer to a 1 litre baking dish, then cover with a double-layer of plastic film and freeze for at least 3-4 hours or overnight.
- Serve scoops of parfait on its own or alongside Roasted Quinces with Cinnamon and Orange on page 229 if desired.

Pikelets with Figs, Honey and Mint

2 free-range eggs, lightly beaten

1 cup milk

50 g unsalted butter, melted, plus extra for cooking

¾ cup plain flour

2 teaspoons baking powder

pinch of salt

4 ripe figs

2 tablespoons chopped mint

freshly ground black pepper

2 tablespoons honey

extra virgin olive oil, for brushing

⅓ cup crème fraîche

1 × 250 g piece honeycomb (optional), to serve

SERVES 4

My favourite way of eating figs is to enjoy them plucked totally ripe, straight from the tree (first making sure that ants haven't invaded, of course). This is when they are at their absolute best. Sadly, this experience is hard to replicate unless you grow your own due to the fragility of ripe figs, which means that commercial growers often pick them before they are ripe so that they can last the distances involved in getting them to the marketplace. For those who don't have their own tree, this is a great dish for bringing out the flavour of bought figs, as the drizzle of honey adds the sweetness that has been robbed by early picking.

I like to make the pikelet batter the night before and leave it in the refrigerator so that it has the chance to thicken properly. These pikelets are so moreish in themselves that you'll find lots of reasons to make them. The freshly ground black pepper adds an element of surprise, while the mint and crème fraîche round the whole dish off.

- Gently whisk eggs, milk and butter in a bowl. Sift flour, baking powder and salt and add to milk mixture in batches, stirring to combine well after each addition. Cover with plastic film and leave to rest in the refrigerator overnight.
- An hour or so before you plan to cook pikelets, cut figs in half and scatter cut sides with mint and a generous grinding of black pepper, then drizzle with 1 tablespoon of the honey. Brush a hot char-grill plate with olive oil, and char-grill figs until caramelised on each side, then set aside.
- Combine crème fraîche with remaining honey and set aside in the refrigerator.
- Place a large non-stick frying pan over medium heat, then melt a knob of butter. Pour 3–4 separate ladlefuls of pikelet mixture into the pan and cook for about 2 minutes or until bubbles appear on the surface, then flip over and cook for another 2 minutes or until lightly golden on the bottom.
- Divide pikelets evenly among 4 plates, top each with 2 grilled fig halves, a spoonful of crème fraîche and a little of the honeycomb, if using, then serve at once.

Chocolate Vino Cotto Pavlova

6 free-range egg whites,
at room temperature

1½ cups caster sugar

¼ cup dutch-process cocoa powder

1 tablespoon vino cotto, plus
extra for drizzling

40 g finely grated dark couverture
chocolate (70 per cent cocoa solids), plus
extra coarsely grated (optional), to serve

extra virgin olive oil, for brushing

5-6 figs, halved or 300 g raspberries

300 ml crème fraîche or double cream

SERVES 6-8

I do love a good pavlova. My talented team at the Farm Shop makes them at the drop of a hat, so when I suggested we try cooking a chocolate one, we were a little surprised to find it needed a process of trial and error to get it right – funnily enough, everyone was happy to be involved and there was no shortage of volunteers for taking the 'failed' ones home. At first I made the error of overdoing the bitter chocolate component, from a texture rather than flavour point of view. Then it was so rich that it needed something to balance it, hence the addition of vino cotto (but balsamic would work equally as well). The result is richness personified. I like my pavlovas gooey in the centre and I love the chocolatey molten mass, but if you prefer a drier meringue, leave it in the turned-off oven with the door slightly ajar until there is no heat left at all in either the oven or meringue.

I pile raspberries onto the cream at the height of summer, when they are at their very best. However, if I make this in late autumn and it's hotter than we expect, raspberries will be well past their prime, so I use beautiful fresh figs instead – like with all my cooking, it's about going with the seasonal flow.

- Preheat conventional oven to 180°C (350°F).
- Line a 24 cm baking tray with baking paper. Draw a 23 cm circle on the paper, then set aside.
- Beat egg whites in a dry, clean bowl with hand-held electric beaters until soft peaks form. Slowly beat in sugar, a spoonful at a time, continuing to beat until the meringue is stiff and shiny. Stir the cocoa into the vino cotto. Then, sprinkle chopped chocolate over the meringue and gently fold the cocoa and vino cotta through the meringue taking care not to knock out too much air from the mixture.
- Mound meringue mixture onto the baking paper within the marked circle, then smooth the sides and top with a spatula. Place baking tray on the centre shelf of the oven, then immediately reduce temperature to 150°C (300°F) and cook for 60-75 minutes. The pavlova should be crisp around the edges and dry on top, but when you prod the centre it should feel 'squidgy'. Turn oven off, open the door slightly, then leave meringue to cool completely in the oven.
- Brush a hot char-grill pan with olive oil, then quickly grill fig halves, cut-sides down, until lightly caramelised and grill marks appear. Remove from heat and leave to cool.
- Invert meringue onto a large, flat plate. Pile cream over centre of meringue, then place figs over the top and drizzle with vino cotto (or use fresh raspberries instead if they are in season). Scatter with coarsely grated chocolate if you like, then serve.

Mango Salad with Mint, Labna, Pink Peppercorns and Ginger Wine

2 cups Greek-style yoghurt

2 green mangoes, peeled, halved and cut into julienne

½ cup Stones Green Ginger Wine

pinch of salt

2 tablespoons caster sugar

2 ripe mangoes, peeled, halved and thickly sliced

extra virgin olive oil, for brushing

¼ cup thinly sliced mint, plus extra to serve

2 teaspoons dried pink peppercorns, very lightly crushed

SERVES 4

Labna is a fresh Middle Eastern cheese made by straining the whey from cow's, goat's or sheep's yoghurt. It is very easy to make at home but needs to be started a day in advance of when you plan to serve it to allow the yoghurt to drain. It can be used in both sweet and savoury dishes.

- Place yoghurt in a sieve or wrapped in a piece of muslin or a clean Chux over a bowl, then leave to drain overnight in the refrigerator. Discard the whey that collects in the bowl; the drained yoghurt curds are called labna. Roll into a ball then refrigerate until needed.

- Place green mango in a bowl with ginger wine and salt, then set aside.

- Sprinkle sugar over sliced ripe mangoes, then toss to combine. Leave to stand for 5–10 minutes. Heat a char-grill pan, then lightly brush with olive oil. Working in batches, cook mango slices on char-grill plate until caramelised on both sides. Leave to cool a little.

- Toss caramelised mango with green mango mixture, mint and peppercorns, then divide among 4 bowls and serve topped with a little of the labna and thinly sliced mint.

Sticky Bananas and French Toast

2 free-range eggs

¾ cup milk

½ teaspoon ground cinnamon

2 thick slices good-quality white bread (I use a freshly baked square milk loaf from Apex Bakery)

unsalted butter, for cooking

2 ripe large bananas (or 3 ripe lady finger bananas), sliced on the diagonal

lemon juice, to taste

extra virgin olive oil, for cooking

icing sugar, to serve

SERVES 2

Pan-fry some bananas in butter and I'm immediately transported back to my childhood. Sometimes Mum would serve these to us for a special breakfast or Sunday night tea, and we loved them. I would almost go so far as to say that this was the only way I'd deign to eat bananas as a child.

Nowadays, we have so many banana varieties to choose from. I've discovered that I absolutely love ripe lady finger bananas either raw or cooked. One of the things I really love about filming my television show is that it gives me the opportunity to meet so many producers and suppliers and to learn continually in the process. It was during a recent trip to Adelaide's Pooraka Market that I first learnt that lady finger bananas are even better when their skins have black markings, something I had previously associated with over-ripe bananas. (However, if you do end up with these, just freeze them in their skins – they make wonderful natural iceblocks for kids.)

- Whisk eggs and milk together, then add cinnamon. Soak bread slices in the egg mixture for a couple of minutes on each side so that they take up some of the liquid but don't become soggy.

- Heat a knob of butter in a frying pan over medium heat, then, when it's sizzling, toss in sliced bananas and cook until caramelised on each side.

- Deglaze the pan with lemon juice, then remove bananas and set aside. Wipe out pan with paper towels.

- Add a little more butter and a splash of olive oil to the clean frying pan and, when it's sizzling, gently place the bread in the pan and cook for 2–3 minutes on each side or until crisp and golden.

- Place a slice of bread on 2 plates. Divide the banana mixture between each plate and dust with a little icing sugar, then serve immediately.

Lime and Coffee Meringues

50 g walnuts

3 free-range egg whites,
at room temperature

120 g caster sugar

25 ml espresso coffee

1 teaspoon finely chopped lime zest

icing sugar (optional), for dusting

COFFEE BUTTER CREAM

50 g caster sugar

45 ml water

125 g unsalted butter, at room
temperature and chopped

2 free-range egg yolks

45 ml espresso coffee

MAKES 12-15

Years ago my friend, Sydney chef Damien Pignolet, wrote a recipe for what he called 'Widow's Kisses' for me on a scrap of paper. Damien told me the story of his friend who had originally given him the recipe, which is now included in his wonderful cookbook, *French*. The recipe incorporated the zest of a 'green' lemon, which I took to mean unripe, so I used lime instead. I have since found out that the French sometimes refer to limes as 'green lemons', and Damien did get the recipe from a Frenchwoman.

I began with Damien's recipe and given my coffee addiction, I added a strong shot of espresso (*ristretto*) to the meringues, which matches the totally addictive coffee butter cream I use to sandwich them together. Although you could use whipped cream instead, this coffee butter cream filling is the icing on the proverbial cake for me.

- Preheat fan-forced oven to 180°C (350°F). Place walnuts on a baking tray and roast for 10 minutes, checking frequently to make sure they don't burn. Immediately wrap in a clean tea towel, then rub to peel off skins. Sift rubbed walnuts through a sieve to get rid of any skins, then leave to cool. Finely chop cooled walnuts and set aside.

- Preheat conventional oven to 100°C (210°F). Line a baking tray with baking paper.

- Beat egg whites with an electric mixer until stiff peaks form, then gradually add the sugar, beating well after each addition. With the motor running, slowly add coffee. Using a metal spoon, fold in walnuts and lime zest. Drop small spoonfuls of the mixture onto the baking paper-lined baking tray, taking care not to handle the meringue mixture too roughly as this will knock out some of the air.

- Bake meringues for 1 hour, then turn the oven off and leave meringues to dry in the oven for 30-40 minutes with the door ajar.

- Meanwhile, for the coffee butter cream, heat sugar and water in a small saucepan over low heat until sugar has dissolved. Bring slowly to the boil over medium heat and cook for 6-8 minutes or until the syrup reaches soft-ball stage. To test, drop a little of the syrup into a glass of cold water, then remove with a teaspoon and knead between your fingertips until it forms a soft ball; if you have a sugar thermometer, it should read 115°C (239°F). Set aside.

- Beat butter with an electric mixer until whipped. Transfer to another bowl and wash and dry the mixing bowl thoroughly. Beat egg yolks in the clean bowl, then, with the motor running, pour the hot sugar syrup over egg yolks in a steady stream and beat until incorporated. Continue to beat for another 5 minutes, then leave to cool. Add whipped butter to the egg mixture and combine, then pour in a little of the coffee at a time, beating thoroughly; adding the coffee slowly prevents the mixture from splitting.

- Just before serving spread a little of the coffee butter cream over the base of a meringue, then sandwich together with another meringue, repeating until all the meringues are sandwiched with butter cream filling.

- Lightly dust meringues with icing sugar just before serving, if desired.

Roasted Quince with Cinnamon and Orange

1.5 kg quinces, peeled, cored, cut into eighths and cores and peel reserved

juice of 2 lemons

600 ml water

1 orange, zest removed in wide strips with a potato peeler, plus juice

400 g caster sugar

1 stick cinnamon

double cream or Brown Sugar and Vino Cotto Parfait (see recipe page 218), to serve

SERVES 6

Quinces are part of my very being. I can't believe I didn't know about them until I came to live in the Barossa as they are one of my favourite foods of all. So it is that in every cookbook I've now written I've included a recipe for quince (and it will always be so).

The key to cooking quince is to do it long and slow so that the amazing transformation in colour from pale-cream to pinky-orange to red and then eventually deep-crimson can occur. It only happens over time but the glorious change in colour is the reward for your patience.

I find that the flavours of orange and cinnamon work wonderfully well here. I'm always open to the possibility of adding a little lemon juice towards the end if I find it too sweet. However, I don't make this part of the recipe as everyone has a different tolerance to sweet things, plus the variety and ripeness of quinces can vary so much, affecting how much sugar is required.

- Preheat conventional oven to 90°C (194°F).
- Squeeze quince pieces with lemon juice to avoid browning. Wrap and tie quince peel and cores in a piece of muslin, then place in a stainless steel saucepan with water, orange juice and zest, sugar and cinnamon. Bring to the boil, then simmer over medium heat for 15 minutes or until syrupy. Remove and discard muslin bag, reserving zest and cinnamon stick.
- Place quince pieces in a shallow baking dish just large enough to fit them all snugly. Add enough syrup (including reserved orange zest and cinnamon stick) to come three-quarters of the way up the sides of the quinces, then cover closely with a piece of baking paper cut to fit the inside of the dish.
- Roast for 8 hours, turning quince pieces occasionally; the quince will become tender and the most beautiful deep ruby colour and the pan juices syrupy. If not, increase the temperature to 120°C (250°F) for the final hour of cooking.
- Serve with double cream or, for something a little more special, the Brown Sugar and Vino Cotto Parfait on page 218.

Candied Ruby Grapefruit

2 large ruby grapefruit, halved widthways

caster sugar, for cooking

MAKES 24 PIECES

These are extremely rich and sweet, so you may want to slice them thinly or toss them in a little caster sugar to serve as sweetmeats. Personally I enjoy eating them in large wedges with no extra sugar added, accompanied by a cup of strong espresso. The candied ruby grapefruit could also be chopped and used instead of the prunes in the recipe for the Chocolate, Almond and Prune Slab on page 191.

These beautiful little morsels don't keep well, as they crystallise when stored, so I only make a small batch at a time.

♦ Using a citrus juicer, squeeze halved grapefruit, leaving the flesh intact and reserving juice for another purpose (I like to have it with my breakfast or with a shot of Campari as an aperitif later in the day).

♦ Cut each grapefruit half into 6 wedges without removing any of the residual flesh. Place wedges in a heavy-based saucepan, then cover with cold water and bring to the boil over high heat. Remove from heat, drain immediately and return to the pan, then cover with cold water and bring to the boil again and drain. Weigh the wedges and measure an equal weight of sugar.

♦ Returned blanched wedges to the same saucepan and add sugar, then place over very low heat (use a simmer mat, if necessary) and stir continuously until sugar dissolves. Cook, stirring occasionally to make sure that the grapefruit doesn't stick to the pan, for 1 hour or until most of the dissolved sugar has been incorporated into the grapefruit and there is no residual stickiness in the base of the pan. Transfer grapefruit wedges to a wire rack placed over a plate to cool and drain for at least a few hours or preferably overnight.

♦ Store candied ruby grapefruit in a sealed jar in the refrigerator, then eat within 2–3 days.

Chocolate Cake with Whisky-soaked Raisins and Orange Zest

⅓ cup raisins

⅓ cup Scotch whisky

160 g blanched almonds

50 g plain flour

375 g dark couverture chocolate
(70 per cent cocoa solids), chopped

finely grated zest of 1 orange

210 g unsalted butter, at room
temperature, chopped

170 g caster sugar

pinch of salt

5 free-range eggs (55 g each),
at room temperature

GANACHE

175 ml pouring cream

250 g dark couverture chocolate
(70 per cent cocoa solids), chopped

SERVES 8

In my Pheasant Farm restaurant days I used to make two beautiful chocolate cakes, the recipes for which I found in Simone Beck's, *Simca's Cuisine* and *New Menus from Simca's Cuisine*. These two cookbooks are so well-thumbed and food-stained – a testament to just how important they were to me at that time.

After a trip to Kennedy & Wilson chocolates in Victoria's Yarra Valley, I revisited my repertoire of chocolate cakes. I decided to pull together everything I had learnt about making them from Simone Beck, and this sumptuous cake is the result. The addition of fresh orange zest lifts both the whisky and raisins, making for a truly decadent cake. Once again, the better the chocolate you use, the better the cake will be.

- Soak raisins in whisky for a few hours to hydrate.
- Preheat fan-forced oven to 180°C (350°F).
- Place almonds on a baking tray and roast for 10 minutes or until golden. Leave to cool slightly, then process in a food processor until finely ground. Add flour and set aside.
- Melt chocolate in a heatproof bowl placed over a saucepan of simmering water, taking care that the bowl doesn't touch the water. Add orange zest to melted chocolate, then stir to combine.
- Beat butter, sugar and salt with hand-held electric beaters until pale and fluffy. Add eggs, one at a time, beating well after adding each one; the mixture will split, but don't worry as it will come together when the almonds and flour are added. Fold in melted chocolate mixture, then soaked raisins. Sprinkle over ground almond and flour mixture and fold to just combine, taking care not to over-mix.
- Lightly grease and line a 20 cm round cake tin with baking paper, then pour mixture into the tin.
- Bake for 1 hour or until a skewer inserted in the centre comes out clean; check in the last 10 minutes of cooking to make sure that a crust doesn't form on the top.
- Remove cake from the oven and place the cake tin on a wire rack to cool for 10 minutes. Carefully turn out cake and leave cake to cool on a wire rack.
- Meanwhile, for the ganache, heat cream in a heavy-based saucepan over medium heat until it comes to the boil. Pour hot cream over chopped choc-olate in a heatproof bowl, then leave for a few minutes to melt. Swirl the bowl to combine cream and chocolate, then pour over the cooled cake to cover evenly. Leave to cool for 1 hour in a cool place (not the refrigerator) before serving.
- Cut the cooled chocolate cake into slices and serve.

Apple and Olive Oil Pudding

3 free-range eggs, separated

125 g caster sugar

75 g plain flour

½ teaspoon baking powder

¼ cup extra virgin olive oil

icing sugar (optional), for dusting

POACHED APPLES

2 large granny smith or pink lady apples, peeled, cored and chopped (to yield about 250 g)

1 cup verjuice

1 tablespoon finely chopped rosemary

1 teaspoon extra virgin olive oil

SERVES 6-8

This is a perfect example of how a recipe can be used like a road map, with many twists and turns taken along its way. Its journey began in early 2000 when I was writing *Maggie's Table* and I was smart enough to have my talented former apprentice and now established chef (as well as writer, farmer and artist), Sophie Zalokar, fly over from Western Australia to help with cooking for the photography. Sophie made the first incarnation of this, an apple tea cake with a caramelised verjuice syrup.

As is so often the case, ideas just bloom, so in 2006 and with the help of the talented Gill Radford, another Barossan, we used the idea of apples and verjuice together again, but with the addition of a fresh and grassy extra virgin olive oil, which added both moistness and flavour. The rosemary was the final addition. I might add that I am now in love with pink lady apples, both for cooking and eating, so if you have them to hand, try them in this – you won't be disappointed.

- For the poached apples, place all the ingredients in a saucepan and bring to the boil over high heat. Reduce heat to low and simmer for 10 minutes or until tender. Drain apples, reserving the poaching liquid, and transfer to a buttered round 20 cm pudding basin or baking dish.

- Preheat fan-forced oven to 180°C (350°F).

- Using hand-held electric beaters, beat egg yolks with half of the sugar until the mixture is pale. In a separate bowl, using clean beaters, whisk egg whites with remaining sugar until soft peaks form.

- Add sifted flour and baking powder to the bowl with egg yolks. Add ¼ cup of the reserved poaching liquid with the olive oil. Using a large metal spoon, gently fold in one-third of the egg whites at a time until well combined. Pour mixture over apples, then bake for 20-25 minutes or until a skewer inserted in the centre comes out clean; the mixture will rise a little like a soufflé and fall back again.

- Serve the apple and olive pudding straight from the baking dish, dusted with a little icing sugar, if desired.

Thank you

I often have to pinch myself when I think how lucky I am in life. Living where I do in the Barossa, I am surrounded by beautiful countryside, my family and community, and so many people who help me so much in all that I do, but particularly in pulling this book together.

Maggie's Kitchen would never have come about if I hadn't begun working with my friend Simon Bryant, whose cheeky, dry sense of humour has always cracked me up. Each day we work together is a totally new adventure as we learn from each other. For that, I also thank the very clever Margot Phillipson, who has become a special friend over the years, as well as her wonderful team, who are such a joy to work with.

Working with Gill Radford, caterer extraordinaire and fellow passionate cook, has been such a bonus. So often a recipe starts off as a kernel of an idea of mine, and then Gill and I will bounce ideas back and forth, leading to the first trial in the kitchen. Even though I sometimes change the recipe substantially at the last moment, the energy of working with Gill during the past few years has made my life as easy as it could be, not least because we are both driven by the imperative to find fresh ideas for using the seasonal produce that is so central to what I do.

The quite amazing Julie Gibbs, my publisher and great friend, knows me so well that she intuitively guides me to what I will be happy with – something that is not quite as easy as one might imagine. I truly don't think there is anyone in the publishing field quite like her, and once again, I often reflect on just how lucky I am to have her belief in me. How lovely it's been to work with my editor Kathleen Gandy again, so particular and correct as she reins in my haphazard style to make as sure as we possibly can that any cook, from a rank beginner to a dab-hand, can tackle every dish in this book with confidence.

Two exceptional young men have conributed greatly to this book. Firstly, my friend Simon Griffiths, whose photographs add so much to my food that just flipping through these pages makes me hungry. Working with Simon again, with our shared history of food, friends and photographs from as far back as our wonderful Tuscan adventures in 1995, has been nothing short of a delight, and I relish the ease with which we work together.

The second exceptional young man is Daniel New, the incredibly talented designer who was responsible for designing my last book, *Maggie's Harvest*. I'll never forget the moment when Julie presented me with the first copy of that book months before it was released. I was truly moved to tears by its beauty and, as a result, Daniel has a very special place in my publishing history. To have his vibrant energy now poured into *Maggie's Kitchen* has been a privilege.

There are of course many more in the team at Penguin, all of whom add so much to the sum of the parts, including production controller Sue Van Velsen and the lovely Erin Langlands.

And in talking of teams, there is mine at the Farm Shop, including Marieanne Pledger, with her wonderful eye for finding memorabilia to use for photography; Dianne Wooldridge, the organiser in the background who is always assisting, including bringing in her grandmother's crockery for photography – as did Lynda Tucker, our own earth mother, always there dispensing love and charm; Fiona Roberts and Andrew Heathfield, who helped on some of the photo shoots; and finally, the rest of the Farm Shop team who, whilst not involved in pulling the book together, gave so much by being the warmest, most hospitable and knowledgeable 'front of house' people ever.

And finally, to my audience and readers – this book is for you.

Thank you all.

Index

A

almonds
Almond affogato 213
Broccoli with almonds and lemon butter 48
Chocolate, almond and prune slab 191
Pot-roasted lamb shoulder with green olives, almonds
and apricots 164
Sicilian rice pudding 206
anchovies
Anchovy butter 155
buying 16
using leftovers 16
apples
Apple and olive oil pudding 235
Apple and prune stuffing for turkey 178
Baked apples 192
Poached apples 235
Pot-roasted pheasant with apples and Calvados 144
Spicy pork and apple pasties 148
asparagus
Asparagus and leek tart 92
Asparagus with soft-boiled eggs and Parmigiano Reggiano 54
Barley risotto with asparagus and fresh goat's curd 161
trimming 54
avocado
Verjuice and avocado jellies 82

B

bain marie (water bath) 28
baking equipment 5
bananas
Sticky bananas and French toast 224
Barley risotto with asparagus and fresh goat's curd 161
beans, dried
Boston baked beans 162
Béchamel sauce 121
beef
Beef in the Italian style 124
Beef pie mix 174
Beef tagine with dried fruit 147
Meatloaf with tomato sugo 167
My spag bog 112
Slow-cooked beef fillet with crushed black pepper
and balsamic 124
Steak and oyster pies 152
Steak sandwiches with skirt steak 150
beetroot
Beetroot, pear and celery heart salad 67
Kangaroo fillet with beetroot and anchovy butter 155
Salad of beetroot, blood orange and pumpkin 36
blind baking 16
blood oranges
Blood orange confit 184
Chocolate ganache tart with blood orange 184
Salad of beetroot, blood orange and pumpkin 36
Boston baked beans 162
bread
Cauliflower with toasted crumbs 40
Sticky bananas and French toast 224
Whole roasted red onions with buffalo mozzarella and
'pulled' bread 168
see also sandwiches
broad beans
Broad beans with pecorino 67
Spring salad 56
Broccoli with almonds and lemon butter 48
broccolini
Orecchiette with rapini, broccolini, cauliflower and pecorino 43

Brown sugar and vino cotto parfait 218
butter
Anchovy butter 155
'nut-brown' 16
Preserved lemon butter 46
Preserved lemon and tarragon butter 109
unsalted 16
Verjuice butter sauce 158

C

cakes
Chocolate cake with whisky-soaked raisins and orange zest 232
Chocolate and hazelnut roulade 199
Génoise sponge 186
Sultana cake 213
Camel scotch fillet marinated in lilly pilly 100
Candied ruby grapefruit 230
capers
Kingfish with roasted tomatoes, capers and olives 110
Warm squid, leek and caper salad 127
capsicum
Rouille 84
caramelised garlic 16
Caramelised lemons 156
Caramelised onions 150
Caramelised radicchio 140
Carrots in verjuice with goat's cheese and pine nuts 60
cauliflower
Cauliflower with toasted crumbs 40
Orecchiette with rapini, broccolini, cauliflower and pecorino 43
Cavolo nero 43
celery
Beetroot, pear and celery heart salad 67
Char-grilled lamb 97
Cheddar, quince and walnut mille-feuille 194
cheese
Asparagus with soft-boiled eggs and Parmigiano
Reggiano 54
Baked savoury cheesecake 78
Barley risotto with asparagus and fresh goat's curd 161
Broad beans with pecorino 67
Carrots in verjuice with goat's cheese and pine nuts 60
Cheddar, quince and walnut mille-feuille 194
Coeur à la crème 202
Eggplant, roasted tomato and 'rag' pasta with
buffalo mozzarella 76
Haloumi and citrus lentils 64
Macaroni cheese 170
Mango salad with mint, labna, pink peppercorns
and ginger wine 224
Mozzarella with crème fraîche and figs – my take on burrata 51
Mozzarella sandwiches 34
My version of pashka – an Easter dessert 208
Orecchiette with rapini, broccolini, cauliflower
and pecorino 43
Parmigiano Reggiano 24
Peanut butter pie 216
Pumpkin, walnut, cheese and verjuice terrine 44
Ricotta, honey and pears 191
Whole roasted red onions with buffalo mozzarella and
'pulled' bread 168
cherries
Poached cherries 214
chestnuts
Chestnut purée dessert 206
Glazed chestnuts 178
chicken livers
My spag bog 112
Warm salad of guinea fowl with orange, livers and walnuts 81
chicken
Chicken braised with figs, honey and vinegar 130
Chicken, grape and Champagne pies 106

Chook legs with vino cotto or balsamic 94
Golden chicken stock 27
Honey and lemon chicken drummettes 122
Roast Barossa chook with preserved lemon and
    tarragon butter 109
roasting 16
Spatchcock in a fig 'bath' 98
Warm smoked chook salad with mustard apricots and
    nicola potatoes 70
chocolate
Chestnut Purée Dessert 206
Chocolate, almond and prune slab 191
Chocolate cake with whisky-soaked raisins and orange zest 232
Chocolate and dried pear 'brownie' 205
Chocolate ganache 184, 206, 232
Chocolate ganache tart with blood orange 184
Chocolate and hazelnut roulade 199
Chocolate vino cotto pavlova 222
couverture 16
Peanut butter pie 216
chopping boards 6
citrus fruit
Haloumi and citrus lentils 64
zest 16, 19
see also lemons; oranges; preserved lemon; ruby grapefruit
Coeur à la crème 202
coffee
Almond affogato 213
Coffee butter cream 226
Coffee jelly 188
confit
Blood orange confit 184
Confit of rabbit with pancetta, pine nuts and raisins 142
Tuna confit with vine leaves 176
cooking times 19
cooking tips 15–28
Crème fraîche parfait 205
crumble
Rhubarb crumble 196
Cucumber gazpacho 54
custard
Baked vanilla custard with coffee jelly 188
base for ice cream 19
rescuing 19
Sabayon 186

D
dates
Honey date relish 100
dressings
Vinaigrette 36, 70, 176
dried fruit
Beef tagine with dried fruit 147
Fruit Mince 210
Fruit Slice 210
Honey date relish 100
My version of pashka – an Easter dessert 208
dumplings
Golden syrup dumplings 214

E
eggs
Asparagus with soft-boiled eggs and Parmigiano Reggiano 54
egg whites 20
freezing egg whites 20
freshness test 19
Perfect omelette with baked mushrooms 48
separating 19
soft-boiling 54
storage 19
eggplant
char-grilling 19

Eggplant pickle 74
Eggplant, roasted tomato and 'rag' pasta with
    buffalo mozzarella 76
Lamb moussaka 121
peeling 19
salting 19
electrical equipment 6
extra virgin olive oil
Apple and olive oil pudding 235
choosing 20

F
figs
Chicken braised with figs, honey and vinegar 130
Chocolate vino cotto pavlova 222
Glazed leg of ham 139
Mozzarella with crème fraîche and figs –
    my take on *burrata* 51
Pikelets with figs, honey and mint 221
Preserved figs 52
Spatchcock in a fig 'bath' 98
fish
buying 13
Crisp-skin salmon with pea salsa 116
Herb-crusted flathead 122
Kingfish with roasted tomatoes, capers and olives 110
Moroccan ocean trout 104
Pan-roasted saltwater barramundi with
    caramelised lemon and rocket 156
Salmon baked with a stuffing of pine nuts, currants and
    preserved lemon wrapped in vine leaves 158
Skate with olives and preserved lemon 109
Smoked ocean trout with potato pikelets 68
Southern herrings in vine leaves 90
Tuna confit with vine leaves 176
freekeh 20, 22, 147, 164,
freezer provisions 9
fruit
buying 11
refrigerating 11
seasonal 12–13
Fruit mince 210
Fruit slice 210

G
garlic, caramelised 16
gelatine leaves
soaking 23
in verjuice 23
Génoise sponge 186
Globe artichokes with pastry and preserved lemon 46
Gluten-free pastry 148, 174
gnocchi
Potato gnocchi with prawns 134
Golden syrup dumplings 214
grapes
Chicken, grape and Champagne pies 106
Sultana cake 213
guinea fowl
Warm salad of guinea fowl with orange, livers and walnuts 81

H
Haloumi and citrus lentils 64
ham
Glazed leg of ham 139
hazelnuts
Brown sugar and vino cotto parfait 218
Chocolate and hazelnut roulade 199
herbs
Grilled octopus in herb paste with rouille 84
herb garden 13
Herb-crusted flathead 122

Mango salad with mint, labna, pink peppercorns and
ginger wine 224
Pikelets with figs, honey and mint 221
Preserved lemon and tarragon butter 109
Roast Barossa chook with preserved lemon and
tarragon butter 109
seasonal 12
Heritage tomato salad 39
honey
Chicken braised with figs, honey and vinegar 130
Honey date relish 100
Honey and lemon chicken drummettes 122
Oat, buttermilk and honey pancakes 78
Pikelets with figs, honey and mint 221
Ricotta, honey and pears 191

J
jellies
Coffee jelly 188
Oyster shooters 52
Raspberry jelly 186
Verjuice and avocado jellies 82

K
Kangaroo fillet with beetroot and anchovy butter 155
Kibbeh 136
kitchen equipment 5-6
kitchen garden
herbs 13
trees 13
knives and slicers 5

L
lamb
Char-grilled lamb 97
Kibbeh 136
Lamb moussaka 121
Meatloaf with tomato sugo 167
Porterhouse of Suffolk lamb with caramelised radicchio 140
Pot-roasted lamb shoulder with green olives, almonds
and apricots 164
Lard Pastry 152
larder (dry goods) 9
leeks
Asparagus and leek tart 92
Warm squid, leek and caper salad 127
lemons
Caramelised lemons 156
Honey and lemon chicken drummettes 122
Meyer lemon curd and raspberry trifle 186
Meyer lemon posset 192
see also preserved lemon
lentils
Haloumi and citrus lentils 64
Lime and coffee meringues 226

M
Macaroni cheese 170
Maggie's prawn cocktail 56
Mango salad with mint, labna, pink peppercorns and ginger wine 224
marinades, post-cooking 24, 97, 115
mayonnaise
Rocket mayonnaise 150
meat
cooking 23
post-cooking marinades 24, 97, 115
resting 23
see also beef; camel; chicken; guinea fowl; ham;
kangaroo; lamb; pheasant; pork; quail; rabbit; veal
Meatloaf with tomato sugo 167
meringue
Chocolate vino cotto pavlova 222
Lime and coffee meringues 226
whisking egg whites 20
mixing bowls 6
Moroccan ocean trout 104
moussaka
Lamb moussaka 121
mozzarella
Eggplant, roasted tomato and 'rag' pasta with
buffalo mozzarella 76
Mozzarella with crème fraîche and figs - my take on burrata 51
Mozzarella sandwiches 34
mushrooms
Perfect omelette with baked mushrooms 48
Soft polenta with sautéed mushrooms 103
Mussels in tomato sugo 97

N
nuts
freezing 23
removing skin 23-4
roasting 23-4
seasonal 12-13
storing 23
see also almonds; hazelnuts; pine nuts; walnuts

O
Oat, buttermilk and honey pancakes 78
olives
Kingfish with roasted tomatoes, capers and olives 110
Olive tart 62
Pot-roasted lamb shoulder with green olives, almonds and
apricots 164
Skate with olives and preserved lemon 109
olive oil, extra virgin 20
omelettes
pans for 48
Perfect omelette with baked mushrooms 48
onions
Caramelised onions 150
Whole roasted red onions with buffalo mozzarella
and 'pulled' bread 168
oranges
Warm salad of guinea fowl with orange, livers and walnuts 81
Orecchiette with rapini, broccolini, cauliflower and pecorino 43
oven 5
Oyster shooters 52

P
pancakes
Oat, buttermilk and honey pancakes 78
panna cotta
Vanilla bean panna cotta 214
parfait
Brown sugar and vino cotto parfait 218
Crème fraîche parfait 205
Passionfruit parfait 200
paschka
My version of paschka - an Easter dessert 208
Passionfruit parfait 200
pasta
dried 24
Eggplant, roasted tomato and 'rag' pasta with
buffalo mozzarella 76
Fresh 76
Macaroni cheese 170
making 24
My spag bog 112
Orecchiette with rapini, broccolini, cauliflower
and pecorino 43
Spaghetti with crab 39
pastries
blind baking 16

Cheddar, quince and walnut mille-feuille 194
Globe artichokes with pastry and preserved lemon 46
Gluten-free pastry 148, 174
Lard pastry 152
making 24
Sour-cream pastry 92
Spicy pork and apple pasties 148
Sweet pastry 174
see also pies; tarts
pavlova
Chocolate vino cotto pavlova 222
peaches
Meyer lemon curd and raspberry trifle 186
Peanut butter pie 216
pears
Beetroot, pear and celery heart salad 67
Chocolate and dried pear 'brownie' 205
Ricotta, honey and pears 191
peas
Frozen pea salsa 116
Frozen pea soup 73
pheasant
Pot-roasted pheasant with apples and Calvados 144
pickles *see* relishes and pickles
pies
Beef pie mix 174
Chicken, grape and Champagne pies 106
Peanut butter pie 216
Steak and oyster pies 152
pikelets
Pikelets with figs, honey and mint 221
Potato pikelets 68
pine nuts
Carrots in verjuice with goat's cheese and pine nuts 60
Confit of rabbit with pancetta, pine nuts and raisins 142
Salmon baked with a stuffing of pine nuts, currants and
preserved lemon wrapped in vine leaves 158
polenta
Soft polenta with sautéed mushrooms 103
pork
Boston baked beans 162
Meatloaf with tomato sugo 167
My spag bog 112
Pork belly in shiraz 128
Slow-cooked Berkshire pork shoulder in milk 179
Spicy pork and apple pasties 148
see also ham
potatoes
Braised waxy potatoes 68
floury 24
Potato gnocchi with prawns 134
Potato pikelets 68
Spring salad 56
Warm smoked chook salad with mustard apricots
and nicola potatoes 70
waxy 24
Pot-roasted lamb shoulder with green olives,
almonds and apricots 164
Pot-roasted pheasant with apples and Calvados 144
Pot-roasted rabbit with prunes and mustard 133
pots and pans 6
Potted prawns 59
Preserved figs 52
preserved lemon
Globe artichokes with pastry and preserved lemon 46
Lamb moussaka 121
Preserved lemon butter 46
Preserved lemon and tarragon butter 109
Roast barossa chook with preserved lemon and
tarragon butter 109
Salmon baked with a stuffing of pine nuts, currants and
preserved lemon wrapped in vine leaves 158

Skate with olives and preserved lemon 109
Spicy Pork and Apple Pasties 148
prunes
Apple and prune stuffing for turkey 178
Chocolate, almond and prune slab 191
Pot-roasted rabbit with prunes and mustard 133
pumpkin
Macaroni cheese 170
Pumpkin, walnut, cheese and verjuice terrine 44
Salad of beetroot, blood orange and pumpkin 36

Q

quail
Barbecued quail 115
Quince-glazed quail 173
quince
Cheddar, quince and walnut mille-feuille 194
Quince-glazed quail 173
Roasted quince with cinnamon and orange 229

R

rabbit
Confit of rabbit with pancetta, pine nuts and raisins 142
Pot-roasted rabbit with prunes and mustard 133
radicchio
Caramelised radicchio 140
Radicchio risotto 118
rapini
Orecchiette with rapini, broccolini, cauliflower and pecorino 43
ras el hanout 104
raspberries
Chocolate vino cotto pavlova 222
Meyer lemon curd and raspberry trifle 186
refrigerator 5
relishes and pickles
Eggplant pickle 74
Honey date relish 100
Saffron tomato relish 73
Rhubarb crumble 196
rice
for risotto 27
Radicchio risotto 118
Sicilian rice pudding 206
Ricotta, honey and pears 191
risotto
Barley risotto with asparagus and fresh goat's curd 161
Radicchio risotto 118
rice for 27
Roast Barossa Chook with Preserved Lemon
and Tarragon Butter 109
rocket
Pan-roasted saltwater barramundi with
caramelised lemon and rocket 156
Rocket mayonnaise 150
Rouille 84
ruby grapefruit
Candied ruby grapefruit 230

S

Sabayon 186
Saffron tomato relish 73
salads
Beetroot, pear and celery heart salad 67
Heritage tomato salad 39
Salad of beetroot, blood orange and pumpkin 36
Spring salad 56
Warm salad of guinea fowl with orange, livers and walnuts 81
Warm smoked chook salad with mustard apricots
and nicola potatoes 70
Warm squid, leek and caper salad 127
salsa
Frozen pea salsa 116

sandwiches
  Mozzarella sandwiches 34
  Steak sandwiches with skirt steak 150
sauces
  Béchamel sauce 121
  Tomato sugo 167
  Verjuice butter sauce 158
seafood
  buying 13
  Grilled octopus in herb paste with rouille 84
  Grilled squid au naturel 90
  Maggie's prawn cocktail 56
  Mussels in tomato sugo 97
  Oyster shooters 52
  Potato gnocchi with prawns 134
  Potted prawns 59
  Spaghetti with crab 39
  Steak and oyster pies 152
  Stuffed oven-baked squid 162
  Warm squid, leek and caper salad 127
  see also fish
semolina
  Grilled semolina 130
Sicilian rice pudding 206
slices
  Fruit slice 210
Slow-cooked beef fillet with crushed black pepper and balsamic 124
Slow-cooked Berkshire pork shoulder in milk 179
Smoked ocean trout with potato pikelets 68
soup
  Cucumber gazpacho 54
  Frozen pea soup 73
Sour-cream pastry 92
Spaghetti with crab 39
Spatchcock in a fig 'bath' 98
spice larder 9
Spring salad 56
Steak and oyster pies 152
Steak sandwiches with skirt steak 150
sterilising jars 27
stock
  Golden chicken stock 27
sugar syrup 27
Sultana cake 213
Sweet pastry 174

T
tagine
  Beef tagine with dried fruit 147
tarts
  Asparagus and leek tart 92
  Baked savoury cheesecake 78
  Chocolate ganache tart with blood orange 184
  Globe artichokes with pastry and preserved lemon 46
  Olive tart 62
terrine
  Pumpkin, walnut, cheese and verjuice terrine 44
tomatoes
  Eggplant, roasted tomato and 'rag' pasta with buffalo mozzarella 76
  Heritage tomato salad 39
  Kingfish with roasted tomatoes, capers and olives 110
  Meatloaf with tomato sugo 167
  Mussels in tomato sugo 97
  Saffron tomato relish 73
  Tomato sugo 167
trays 6
trifle
  Meyer lemon curd and raspberry trifle 186
Tuna confit with vine leaves 176
Turkey with apple and prune stuffing and glazed chestnuts 178

U
utensils, small 6

V
Vanilla bean panna cotta 214
Veal cutlets with garlic 136
vegetables
  cooking 27
  seasonal 12-13
verjuice
  Carrots in verjuice with goat's cheese and pine nuts 60
  gelatine in 23
  Oyster shooters 52
  Pumpkin, walnut, cheese and verjuice terrine 44
  Verjuice and avocado jellies 82
  Verjuice butter sauce 158
vine leaves
  Pumpkin, walnut, cheese and verjuice terrine 44
  Salmon baked with a stuffing of pine nuts, currants and preserved lemon wrapped in vine leaves 158
  Southern herrings in vine leaves 90
  Tuna confit with vine leaves 176

W
walnuts
  Cheddar, quince and walnut mille-feuille 194
  Pumpkin, walnut, cheese and verjuice terrine 44
  Warm salad of guinea fowl with orange, livers and walnuts 81
water bath (bain marie) 28
Whole roasted red onions with buffalo mozzarella and 'pulled' bread 168

Z
zucchini
  Spring salad 56
  Zucchini flowers 64

Bibliography

Alexander, Stephanie and Beer, Maggie, *Stephanie Alexander and Maggie Beer's Tuscan Cookbook* (Penguin, Melbourne, 2003)

Beck, Simone, *New Menus from Simca's Cuisine* (Harcourt Brace Jovanovich, New York, 1979)

Beck, Simone, *Simca's Cuisine* (Knopf Random House, New York, 1972)

Beer, Maggie, *Maggie's Harvest* (Lantern Penguin, Melbourne, 2007)

Beer, Maggie, *Maggie's Table* (Lantern Penguin, Melbourne, 2005)

David, Elizabeth, *French Provincial Cooking* (Penguin, London, 1970)

Kyritsis, Janni, *Wild Weed Pie* (Lantern Penguin, Melbourne, 2006)

Pignolet, Damien, *French* (Lantern Penguin, Melbourne, 2005)

LANTERN

Published by the Penguin Group
Penguin Group (Australia)
707 Collins Street, Melbourne, Victoria 3008, Australia
(a division of Penguin Australia Pty Ltd)
Penguin Group (USA) Inc.
375 Hudson Street, New York, New York 10014, USA
Penguin Group (Canada)
10 Alcorn Avenue, Toronto, Ontario, Canada M4V 3B2
(a division of Penguin Canada Books Inc.)
Penguin Books Ltd
80 Strand, London WC2R 0RL, England
Penguin Ireland
25 St Stephen's Green, Dublin 2, Ireland
(a division of Penguin Books Ltd)
Penguin Books India Pvt Ltd
11 Community Centre, Panchsheel Park, New Delhi - 110 017, India
Penguin Group (NZ)
67 Apollo Drive, Rosedale, Auckland 0632, New Zealand
(a division of Penguin New Zealand Pty Ltd)
Penguin Books (South Africa) (Pty) Ltd, Rosebank Office Park, Block D,
181 Jan Smuts Avenue, Parktown North, Johannesburg, 2196, South Africa
Penguin (Beijing) Ltd
7F, Tower B, Jiaming Center, 27 East Third Ring Road North,
Chaoyang District, Beijing 100020, China

Penguin Books Ltd, Registered Offices: 80 Strand, London, WC2R 0RL, England

First published by Penguin Group (Australia), 2008
This paperback edition published by Penguin Group (Australia), 2015

13 5 7 9 10 8 6 4 2

Text copyright © Maggie Beer 2008
Photographs copyright © Simon Griffiths 2008
Front cover photograph copyright © Earl Carter 2015

Design by Daniel New © Penguin Group (Australia)
Photography by Simon Griffiths except for front cover by Earl Carter
Photograph on page VII courtesy John Kruger
Typeset in Interstate by Post Pre-press Group, Brisbane, Queensland
Colour reproduction by Splitting Image Colour Studio Pty Ltd, Clayton, Victoria
Printed in China by Everbest Printing Co. Ltd.

National Library of Australia
Cataloguing-in-Publication data:

Beer, Maggie
Maggie's kitchen
9781921382956 (paperback)
Cooking, Australian.
Griffiths, Simon photographer.

641.5

penguin.com.au/lantern